Is Peace Possible in the Holy Land?

Christian Palestinians Speak

The Justice and Peace Commission

This book, released by the Justice and Peace Commission, contains a compelling collection of articles and declarations from Jerusalem that provide an in-depth understanding of who the Christian Palestinians are today, as well as, the viewpoint on the Israel/Palestine conflict emerging from the Christian community. The authors are the members of the Justice and Peace Commission of the Assembly of Catholic Ordinaries in the Holy Land, presided over by Latin Patriarch (emeritus) Michel Sabbah.

Originally published in the Holy Land by the Justice and Peace Commission 2019. U.S. edition adapted by Jeffery Abood with permission 2020. For copies or more information, please contact: in the Holy Land – medialpj@lpj.org or in the U.S. – jabood@att.net.

Contents

Preface

From the Pastoral Letter of
His Beatitude Patriarch Michel Sabbah

The Christians are few in number in this Holy Land and in the Church of Jerusalem. That is not only the result of historical or social circumstances. This reality is linked directly to the mystery of Jesus in this land. Two thousand years ago, Jesus came here and with his apostles, his disciples and the small number of faithful, who believed in him, they also remained few in number. Today, two thousand years later, Jesus remains in the same situation of "not being recognized" in his land; and Jerusalem, the city of redemption and the source of peace for the world, remains a city that has not yet welcomed redemption and that has not yet found its peace. And in this situation, the Christians are a small number of witnesses to Jesus in his land.

To be small in this land is simply to live as Jesus lived here. That does not mean having a diminished life on the margins or a life made up of fear and perplexity. We know why we are small, and we know what place we should occupy in our society and in the world. We are part of the mystery of Jesus, and we remain with him on Calvary, strong and supported by the hope and the joy of the Resurrection, which are to be lived and shared with all.

Jesus told us that the mustard seed is small, but it grows and becomes a tree, and "the birds of the air come and make nests in its branches." (Mt 13:31-32) To be small, Jerusalem being the city of redemption and of peace for the world, not for itself – this is what determines the vocation of every Christian in this Holy Land: a vocation to be a witness, a vocation to lead a difficult life, today because of the political conflict, and tomorrow because the Christian's life will remain a permanent battle in order to be good salt, useful leaven, a light in society and a redemption that is fulfilled day by day in the mystery of God.

Every society counts on the number of its citizens, its soldiers, and on the quantity of its weapons. We Christians, with or without numbers, count first of all on the faith of each one of us. Jesus says: with faith you can move mountains. The State says: with technology, with a quantity of weapons and of men, it can subdue the earth, open roads and level mountains, but it remains incapable of finding peace. As for us, we keep meditating on the word of Jesus: "If you have faith the size of a mustard seed, you will say to this mountain, 'Move from here to there,' and it will move; and nothing will be impossible for you." (Mt 17:20-21) That is why, while respecting all the useful human means, we try to strengthen and increase our faith in Him in whom we have believed. The small number of Christians must be compensated first of all by faith, and secondly by the formation that makes each Christian necessary in constructing or reconstructing his and her country; and finally, by each Christian becoming aware of his and her responsibility in society and the need for him and her to share all the sacrifices required to construct or reconstruct. This Christian formation is a responsibility of the whole community, not only of those who are the leaders in the Church, for in a community of believers, each person is concerned about each person.

1. Introduction

Who are the Christian Palestinians?

The Holy Land constitutes the cradle of the Christian faith, today divided between two political realities. The first is the State of Israel, established in 1948 on 78% of historical Palestine. The second includes the territories militarily occupied by Israel in the 1967 war, which were claimed by the Palestinians for a future State of Palestine.[1] Here Jesus Christ was born, lived, died and rose from the dead, fulfilling the promises of God to the patriarchs, priests, kings, sages and prophets of ancient Israel who lived in this land. Here too, the first church of believers was established in Jerusalem and from Jerusalem, the apostles set off to preach the Good News to the ends of the earth. The land and its towns echo in churches throughout the world, in the readings from the Old and New Testaments, in liturgy and song. To this land, Christians have

---

[1] Since 2012, many countries, including the Holy See, have recognized a State of Palestine in the territories occupied by Israel in 1967.

come as pilgrims from near and far to renew and deepen their faith at the Holy Places that mark the history of salvation. Since the first half of the first century, the Holy Land has been home to Christian communities, whose members have played a central role in the history of this land. Who are the Christian Palestinians today?

Christian Palestinians belong to a mosaic of different Christian Churches and communities: Byzantine (or Greek) Orthodox and Catholic, Roman (or Latin) Catholic, Maronites, Armenians both Apostolic and Catholic, Syrian Orthodox and Catholic, Copts, Ethiopians, Anglicans, Lutherans and a plethora of other Protestant and Evangelical groups. Due to the tragic history of Palestine in the 20th century, the vast majority of Christian Palestinians live outside historical Palestine, in a far-flung diaspora, stretching from the surrounding Arab countries, particularly Jordan, Lebanon, Syria, Egypt and the Arab Gulf to Europe, North and South America and Australia. The dramatic story continues today as Palestinians continue to struggle against Israeli occupation in the Palestinian Territories and discrimination in the State of Israel and their consequences for Palestinian society.

Within historical Palestine, one can discern two distinct socio-political milieus in which Christian Palestinians live:

- Most Christian Palestinians in the Holy Land are citizens of the State of Israel, living in areas that became part of this state after the armistice agreement of January 1949. Christian Palestinians who are citizens of the State of Israel number around 120,000 today, constituting 75% of the Christian citizens of the State of Israel.[2] Christians comprise just over 2% of the Israeli population.

- Christian Palestinians who reside in the territories that were militarily occupied by Israel during the 1967 War number around 50,000. The Palestinian residents of East Jerusalem carry Israeli identity cards, and the Christian Palestinian population of Jerusalem today is about 10,000, or just over 1% of the total population of the city. In the rest of the West Bank, there are about 39,000 Christian Palestinians, whereas less than 1,000 Christians remain in the Gaza Strip. Christians constitute under 2% of the population in the Palestinian Territories.

---

[2] The other 25% of the Christian population among the citizens of Israel are Christians who are integrated into the Jewish Israeli population the vast majority of whom are immigrants to Israel from the former Soviet Union. In addition, there are about 150,000 Christian migrant workers and asylum seekers who reside in Israel. In addition, throughout the Holy Land, there are small but important communities of expatriate religious, who play an important role in the leadership of the Church and Church institutions.

The identity of Christian Palestinians has been forged in the long centuries of their eventful history in the Holy Land. Each period of history has left distinctive characteristics that continue to forge Christian Palestinian identity today. This history can be divided into seven distinctive periods:

The Martyrdom Period   Martyr, a Greek word that means "witness," might indeed characterize the early Church as it began to bear witness to the Resurrection of Christ and sometimes pay a heavy price for that fidelity. According to the Acts of the Apostles, the Church was founded in Jerusalem on the day of Pentecost, fifty days after Christ rose from the dead. The outpouring of the Holy Spirit on the disciples, who became apostles, pushed them to preach the Good News of Christ's resurrection in Jerusalem, throughout the territory of Palestine and to the furthest extents of the earth. The Church of Jerusalem is the mother Church of the Christian Church throughout the world. The first generations of Christians faced persecution, first from their Jewish brothers, who rejected the Gospel they preached, and then from the Roman authorities in the Empire, who saw the new religion as a threat to established order. Martyrs from the Holy Land are prominent among those who spilt their blood to spread the Gospel. Despite persecution, Christians in the Holy Land contributed much to the early life of the Church, and among them were the Virgin Mary, the apostles, important early Church Fathers (like Justin Martyr from Nablus) and holy men and women throughout the generations.

The Byzantine Period   The period of persecution ended with the Edict of Milan in 313, when Roman Emperor Constantine recognized Christianity as a legitimate religion. From the acceptance of Christianity in the Empire until the Islamic conquest, in the middle of the seventh century, the Holy Land was mostly under Christian rule, except for a brief Persian invasion in the sixth century. It was at this time that the imposing monuments built by Byzantine rulers at the holy sites began to spring up all over the land. At the very center of this prolific building impetus stood the Church of the Resurrection, also known as Holy Sepulchre and containing both the place of the crucifixion and the empty sepulchre that pointed to the figure of Christ. This was also the time of the founding of the first monasteries, in the region of Gaza, as well as in the Judean Desert, which became a teeming oasis of spiritual life. Pilgrims began flowing to the land and were welcomed by the Christians living in the land. Very early on, the various churches of the East and the West, whose members came on pilgrimage, sought to have permanent representation in Jerusalem. Originally, they all recognized the local bishop of Jerusalem as their bishop, but this unity was compromised as a consequence of the

Christological controversies in the 5th century. Those Churches that did not recognize the council of Chalcedon (451) then started establishing separate communities with their own hierarchies, introducing the first divisions in Jerusalem. Among the great figures in the Holy Land of this period are Saint Cyril of Jerusalem, a pre-eminent Church Father, and Saint Sabba, a great figure of Palestinian monasticism.

The Muslim Period   A new religion, Islam that was founded in the Arabian Peninsula, soon spread through the entire Middle East. In 637, the second Caliph, Umar, entered Jerusalem. He was escorted on a visit of the Church of the Resurrection by Patriarch of Jerusalem Sophronios and set in place the pact that would govern relations between Muslims and Christians in the centuries to come, relations based upon rights and respect. The most important transformation in these centuries was that Christians adopted the Arabic language and became more and more integrated into the Arabic culture that spread throughout the Middle East. Over the centuries, Christians became a minority in Palestine and yet maintained an important place in society and contributed greatly to the culture of the Arab world. From this period on, Christian Palestinians have lived as part of a society marked by the Arabic language and culture and the religion of Islam. The challenge has remained to enter into a profound dialogue with Muslims that guarantees the full participation and civic rights of Christians in society. There were periods that were marked by intolerance also. The most noteworthy was the persecution of Christians under the Fatimid Caliph Al-Hakim bi-Amr Allah, who destroyed parts of the Church of the Resurrection (Holy Sepulchre in 1009. Among the prominent figures from the Holy Land in this period were Saint John of Damascus, monk at Mar Saba; Theodor Abu Qura, another monk in the same monastery and an important translator into Arabic; and Abraham of Tiberias.

The Crusader Period　　At the end of the 11th century, the Church in Rome proclaimed a crusade to liberate the Tomb of Christ from the hands of the Muslims. The ensuing two centuries marked a time of European military incursion into the Muslim heartland. In the initial period, Eastern Christians suffered as much as their Muslim neighbors as the Latin invaders did not spare Muslim, Christian or Jew. As a consequence of the division between the Church of Rome and the Church of Constantinople after 1054, the arrival of the Crusaders also led to new tensions and divisions among the Christians in the Holy Land, illustrated by the creation of the Latin Patriarchate in Jerusalem. Ultimately, the Crusaders were unsuccessful and pushed out of the Holy Land, and Muslim rule was re-established. However, even after the end of the

Crusades, the Latin Church remained part of the Church in Palestine under the Franciscan custody of the Holy Land.

The Ottoman Period- In 1517, the Holy Land came under Ottoman rule. By that time, the Ottoman Empire had conquered Constantinople. Soon their empire would stretch through most of North Africa, much of the Middle East and into the Balkans. In this period, the cities in Palestine were the basis of identity. Christians, like Muslims and Jews, identified themselves as being Jerusalemites, Hebronites or coming from Ramleh, Nablus or Tiberias, etc. Although Ottoman rule certainly entrenched Islam as the religion of the Empire, the various religious communities were given a certain degree of autonomy in the administration of their internal affairs and tolerated, providing they did not challenge Ottoman political authority. The religious leadership was accorded the role of representing the entire community. This led to the institutionalization of "confession' (*ta'ifiyyah*) as a fundamental part of one's identity. Christian divisions – Byzantine Orthodox, Byzantine Catholic, Latin, Maronite, etc. – were entrenched as people and identified by the authorities as belonging to a denomination. With the decline of Ottoman rule in the nineteenth century, European powers became more and more involved in the affairs of the Empire and imposed themselves as protectors of different Churches. The French became protectors of the Catholics, both Latin and Eastern rites. The Russians were protectors of the Byzantine Orthodox Churches, and the British and Germans promoted the establishment of Anglican and Lutheran communities. The nineteenth century also saw the expansion of a Christian institutional presence in the Holy Land – the establishment of schools, hospitals, orphanages, etc. The beginnings of an Arab renaissance in the 19th century, often initiated by Christians, would lead to the rise of modern nationalism, in which Christians also took a leading role. This period also saw the beginning of a steady Christian migration towards the countries of the new world and the founding of Christian Palestinian communities in the United States, Latin America and Australia, as well as the beginning of an ever more numerous "diaspora." On the other hand, in the wake of the massacres of Armenians and Syrian Christians towards the end of the Ottoman period, many refugees from these communities found refuge in Palestine.

The British Mandate Period In December 1917, the Ottomans conceded defeat in the Holy Land, and the British took over administration of the country. The League of Nations confided the Holy Land to the British as a mandate. The British instituted a colonial regime in which a certain degree of equality was established among all residents, regardless of religious denomination. The establishment of European-style institutions also intensified. However, the British also aroused the ire of the population by promoting the idea of a "Jewish homeland" in Palestine. In addition, among both Catholic and Orthodox Christians, they were suspect of promoting Anglican and Protestant forms of Christianity. Prominent Christian Palestinians joined with Muslims in the national movement and resisted colonial rule. Among the contributors to the Palestinian national movement as part of a wider Arab sense of belonging were George Antonius, historian of the movement; Khalil al-Sakakini, educator and social activist; and Greek Catholic Archbishop of Galilee, Gregorios Hajjar. The seeds of the present conflict, pitting Palestinian Arab against Israeli Jew have their roots in the policies of the British authorities.

The Modern Period - Palestine, Israel and Jordan   In November 1947, the United Nations formulated resolution 181 that foresaw the partition of Palestine into two states, a Jewish state and an Arab one, with the area of Jerusalem falling under United Nations administration as a *corpus separatum*. In the War that ensued, the resolution was ignored as the newly established State of Israel and the Hashemite Kingdom of Jordan annexed almost all the territory of historical Palestine. About 78% of the territory was incorporated into the State of Israel. In the areas that fell under Israeli rule, hundreds of thousands of Palestinians either fled or were expelled. Since

1948, the vast majority of Christian Palestinians live outside of historical Palestine, and as the tragedy continues, many more have drifted away from their historical homeland because of violence and discrimination. Within the State of Israel, prominent Christian Palestinians have been among the leaders of the Arab minority, struggling for freedom and equality. Christians have been at the forefront of political activity. This includes members of Knesset like Tawfiq Toubi and Azmi Bishara, heads of political associations like Rev. Shehade and Rev. Riah Abu al-Assal, and prominent writers, such as Emil Habibi and Anton Shammas. Christian institutions in the Arab sector in Israel have excelled and have also led the struggle for equality. During the 1967 War, Israel occupied the rest of historical Palestine. In these areas too, Christian Palestinians have joined with Muslims to struggle against occupation and all the woes it brings in its wake. Christian Palestinians engaged themselves fully in the Palestinian national movement to fight the occupation Among these were Father Ibrahim Ayyad, George Habbash, Naif Hawatmeh, Hanan Ashrawi, etc. During this period, the Church leadership was also indigenized to some extent. At this time, the Anglican and Protestant Churches, then the Latin Catholic and other Churches, named Christian Palestinians to serve as their heads. Undoubtedly today, the struggle against the Israeli occupation in the West Bank and Gaza, and for democracy and equality for all citizens of Israel, are very important factors that define the identity and mission of Christian Palestinians.

Christian Palestinians are united by their faith, by their historical experience, by their struggle against occupation and discrimination, by their commitment to justice, peace and equality, and by their hope that one day a definitive and just peace will prevail in the Holy Land, and Palestine will take its rightful place among the nations as a modern, democratic state.

This book presents the aspirations, hopes and struggles of Christian Palestinians, examining the various aspects of their identity and mission today. This discussion includes a presentation of a variety of themes that are necessary to understand this identity and mission:

- *the socio-political and economic context in the Holy Land.*
- *the regional and international context.*
- *relations with Muslims and Jews.*
- *relations with the Christians and the Churches in the rest of the world.*
- *faith, charity and Christian institutions.*
- *the youth.*
- *the question of Jerusalem.*
- *the Christian Palestinian diaspora.*
- *the future of Christian Palestinians.*

The book also includes a collection of statements from the Justice and Peace Commission of the Assembly of Catholic Ordinaries of the Holy Land that deal with issues in the life of the Christian community. The authors of this book are the members of the Commission for Justice and Peace, which serves as a "think tank" to help the Catholic hierarchy, the clergy, the religious and the laity to reflect on issues pertaining to justice and peace in the Catholic dioceses of the Holy Land. It also seeks to raise the consciousness of the Universal Church with regard to issues affecting the Church and the Christian presence in the Holy Land.

2. Christians of the Holy Land and Christians of the World

The Holy Land in which Christian Palestinians are called to live is their historic homeland; however, it is also a land called holy, a land to which all Christians turn their gaze whenever they remember the events of the history of salvation and particularly the life, ministry, death and resurrection of Jesus Christ. This inevitably means that relations between Christian Palestinians and Christians throughout the world, who see the land as a spiritual homeland, are both natural and complex.

The encounter between local Christian Palestinians and expatriate Christians has been an integral part of the life of Christians in the Holy Land since the time of the birth of the Church. At the first Christian Pentecost, a local band of disciples entered into a relationship with pilgrims who had come for the Jewish feast of Pentecost. Some of these pilgrims became believers through the testimony of Saint Peter. This was the beginning of a mission of Christians from the Holy Land to preach the Gospel to the furthest ends of the earth. Since then, the local Church has continued to welcome pilgrims coming to the land from all corners of the planet. However, these pilgrims often solely come to venerate the stones of the Holy Places. Local Christians strongly encourage these to come and encounter the "living stones," the Christian Palestinians as well. Pilgrims are invited to encounter all others who dwell in the land, to become aware that Christians and non-Christians live in a permanent situation of conflict, which has pitted two peoples against one another in the land. This contact with the suffering of the sons and daughters of the land should become an integral part of the pilgrims' prayer, as well as the universal Church's witness and action for the Land of Jesus and all its inhabitants.

Over the centuries, expatriate Christians came to settle around the Holy Places. Some came for reasons of simple piety, but many came as envoys, sent by their Churches, to engage in the work of the Church in the Holy Land. Today, there are many bishops, priests, men and women religious and lay people from foreign lands serving the mission of the Church in the Holy Land. Sometimes, these expatriate Christians learn Arabic, the local language, and begin to identify with the Local Church. In many cases however, they remain isolated in monasteries and religious houses and in institutions and missions where they have little contact with the daily life and preoccupations of the local Church, and continue their day to day lives in Italian, French, English, German, etc. Although there have been moves to indigenize the Church leadership and contextualize Church discourse in the Holy Land so the local Church can live by its proper faith, carry out its own mission, and make its voice heard, this process is long and arduous. Today, the major representative Churches in the Holy Land, which include Greek Orthodox, Armenian and Latin Churches, are all lead by expatriates, even if Christian Palestinians are at the head of smaller Christian communities such as the Anglicans and Lutherans.

The worldviews of local Christians and expatriate Christians are often divergent because of their different backgrounds, histories and loyalties. A conscious dialogue is necessary in order to bridge the gaps, particularly on sensitive subjects like the service of the Church, the political situation and the interreligious dialogue. Christians from Europe and North America often come to the land with definite ideas about how institutions should be administered, how education should be transmitted and how interpersonal relations should function. Local Christians might have very different ideas. Particularly sensitive are the political issues. Christians from post-Holocaust Europe sometimes come to the land with an urgent perception of the need for Jewish-Christian reconciliation. In contrast, local Christians experience the hardships of occupation and discrimination at the hands of a state that defines itself as Jewish. Expatriate Christians might have their own clear concepts of issues, such as inter-religious dialogue, conflict resolution, the struggle for justice and political change. Local Christians might be rooted in an experience that makes these concepts difficult to accept. Dialogue within the Church between local and expatriate Christians is essential to avoid division.

Expatriate Christians established a plethora of institutions throughout the Holy Land, including schools, hospitals, orphanages, homes for the elderly and handicapped, etc. These institutions serve local Christians and have also opened their doors to all inhabitants of the land who search for the services offered. Today, these institutions play a significant role in the mission of the Church. Many local Christians find employment in these institutions and have risen to positions of leadership. Yet again, the delicate issues are how policy in the institutions is set, how resources are distributed and to what extent the voice of local Christians is heard.

The Church of the Holy Land is a Church in need of spiritual, moral, financial and logistic support from the international

Christian community. This relationship of support is rooted in the New Testament when Saint Paul insisted on collecting financial means for the community in Jerusalem. (cf. Romans 15:26, 1 Corinthians 16:3) Today, the generosity of the Universal Church sustains the Church in the Holy Land and its mission. One of the important objectives of this support is to enable Christians to remain in the land of their birth, supporting housing projects, educational institutions, health care facilities, frameworks for the elderly and handicapped, creation of employment, etc. Financial support is intimately linked with deciding policy, especially on how the support is used best. This is another delicate domain where dialogue is essential.

One of the major challenges of the Church in the Holy Land and throughout the Middle East today is the issue of migration. Many Christian Palestinians, whose roots go back to the first community of disciples in Jerusalem, feel alienated in their own land, fear for the future of their children and dream of a better life elsewhere. This situation has many causes, predominantly the political situation in the country, but also certain church attitudes as mentioned elsewhere in this book. The local Church is deeply pained by this reality and fears for the vitality of the local community. Christian Palestinians need the support and understanding of the Universal Church in facing its many challenges. Local Christians should be supported not only in making their lives materially possible but also in facing challenges within both Israeli and Palestinian societies. Within Israeli society, there is the need to oppose discrimination and oppressive political and military measures that make Palestinian life unbearable. On the Israeli side, the issue is political, touching on the viability of stability, equality and justice. Within Palestinian society, a long journey over many centuries has focused on how to coexist with others, collaborate with them and reach complete equality and mutual acceptance. Today, this journey necessitates even more awareness and effort at all levels of Palestinian society. In supporting this struggle to keep local Christians rooted in the Holy Land and promoting a prosperous, healthy community that contributes to the welfare of society, the Universal Church and Christians everywhere can promote the welfare of the Church in the Holy Land, and in particular the cause of justice and peace in Israel-Palestine.

Today, Christians in Palestine and Israel call on the international Christian community to focus on justice and peace in Jerusalem. They call on their brothers and sisters to be aware that Christian Palestinians are living in an abnormal political situation, in a state of hostility between the Land's two peoples, Israelis and Palestinians. Furthermore, they call on them to be aware that Christians in the Holy Land are largely Palestinians and support of them includes making the dream of justice and peace part of their prayer, their action and their pilgrimages. Called not "to forget the poor of Jerusalem," today means to act for justice and peace, to be agents of reconciliation and wellbeing and future of Christians in the Holy Land.

3. The Regional and International Context

The conflict between Palestinians and Israelis has never been limited to a local conflict between two parties. Since the beginning of the conflict, it has had an international dimension. The land itself is at the center of the development of three of the world's most religious traditions: Judaism, Christianity and Islam. Jews, Christians and Muslims, who make up a large part of the world's population, wherever they might be, are not indifferent to what happens in Palestine. The entire Arab world, as well as the Western powers, have been and remain engaged, in one way or another, in this conflict, which has affected and continues to affect the entire region.

It needs to be stated at the outset that the conflict in Palestine and throughout the region is not a religious conflict but rather a conflict over hegemony and influence. Much of what is happening today is a reaction to Western attempts to control the area and decide its fate. Alongside the attempts to end foreign intervention, there is the struggle within the region against social and political injustices due to the lack of freedom on every level, the inequality between rich and poor, the lack of development and the despair of young people. Political mobilization against the woes that originate in foreign lands, as well as those at home, finds energy in radical ideologies. Today the most important of these is religious extremism. It is thus important to understand and critique the causes of the present malaise rather than uniquely condemning the symptoms of the malaise. Religious extremism is not the cause of the malaise but rather an attempt, however reprehensible, to deal with it.

At present, the regional context is primarily a situation of general political and economic instability. An unholy alliance, conscious or unconscious, between Western interests and radical Muslim extremism has achieved overwhelming destruction in the attempt to reshape and thus create a "new Middle East." In this apparent convergence of radical Islam and Western policy, tens of thousands have been killed and millions displaced throughout the region, particularly in Syria and Iraq. Among those who have suffered the consequences have been people of all religions. This includes Christians, Yazidis and Muslims, both Sunni and Shia, as well as Druze and Alawites, too.

The Israeli-Palestinian question remains the key to understanding Western policy applied to the region. The State of Israel came into being with the blessing of the West. The West remains committed to its existence in the region and its defense.

However, in order to survive, the State of Israel must be maintained as the strongest power in the region. Those Arab countries that dared to challenge Israeli hegemony have been destroyed, in particular Iraq, Syria and Egypt. Today only Iran remains as a regional threat for Israel. However, United States policy now seems to pit those in the Arab world against one another. Sunni Saudi Arabia is placed at the center of the conflict against Iran, a Shiite power. Furthermore, focusing uniquely on the so-called "Iranian threat," United States policy makers propose that the conservative Sunni regimes in the Arab Gulf together with the quasi-military regime established in Egypt forge an alliance with Israel to fight the Iranian threat.

Parallel to these developments, and in partial response to them, a radical and intolerant version of Islam has spread among a new generation of Muslims in the Arab Middle East. This ideology condemns the conservative and authoritarian regimes that have been promoted in various ways by Western policy. Many fear that these radical movements act in concert with Israeli intervention and serve as a tool for weakening the Arab world and dividing it. Ultimately, the result will be the destruction of the Middle East as the homeland of a great Islamic-Arab civilization and a mosaic of religious and ethnic communities dwelling within its orbit. With the dramatic rise of ISIS (Islamic State in Iraq and Syria), a type of mystical enthusiasm for death, violence and destruction has and continues to dominate many people. Within this ideology, there is a dream of an Islamic state, strong, powerful, independent. However, the ideology focuses on an even stronger fascination with death that is the imperative to kill the infidel, the non-Muslim as well as the dissenting Muslim, to destroy the vestiges of non-Muslim culture, to annihilate the enemies of Islam both at home and abroad, in the West and, in doing so, to enter "Paradise." The consequences of this death-oriented ideology and the attitudes that allow for its promotion and spread are a palpable threat not only to the Christians in the Middle East, but to the entire Middle East, as well as to the West.

The successful and unsuccessful attempts to overthrow the totalitarian regimes that reigned supreme from Morocco to Iraq, known as the "Arab spring," led to the unexpected emergence of radical Islamic forces that stepped into the power vacuum in many of the countries of the Middle East, especially in Iraq and Syria. After almost a decade of bloodshed and destruction, the Arab world is exhausted and depleted, bleeding, and will need a long time to recover, to regain stability and a normal life. Even if the Islamic radicals have been defeated in Egypt, Syria, Iraq and elsewhere, the calls for reform that resounded during the "Arab spring" have not led to real change. Instead, in addition to the crippling political instability, traditional political, social and religious discourse have remained in place. Anachronistic religious education, based on outdated and irrelevant theses about society, impede change, and the people are no freer today than they were at the outset of the "Arab spring." Yet, their countries are far more impoverished, with infrastructure destroyed and inter-communal relations in a state of deep trauma.

In the countries of the Middle East today, citizens are living under a double threat:

 a. There is an external threat originating in the policies of the West, acting in unison with Israel, that plot out a "new Middle East." This new reality serves the interests of the West and seemingly sees no interest in preserving the plurality of religious, ethnic and cultural communities in the Middle East.

 b. The internal threat is a double one. Firstly, there is the threat unleashed by radical religion that necessitates dealing with the religious questions of 1.) What role does religion play in society and in politics? And 2.) How should the new generations be educated with regard to religious tradition?

Secondly, there is the threat that comes from the inequality in the distribution of wealth and the reality of dire poverty as opposed to great affluence within the societies of the Middle East. An internal struggle of thought and concrete politics is going on in all these countries. There is a need to determine how governments promote, instead of deny, a life of dignity for one and all.

This is the general context in which Christian Palestinians, like all other citizens, live in Palestine/Israel, Jordan and throughout the region. The future of Christians depends upon, and is largely determined by, the future of their countries. Thus far, policies that have been applied have caused the death or forced emigration of millions of people in the Middle East. This includes Christians. The stability and future of one and all depend on the stability and eventual prosperity of these countries.

4. Jerusalem Christians

Christian Palestinians constitute a diminishing part of the population of Jerusalem but are still a vibrant community. This is how one could describe the 8,000 to 9,000 Christians living in Jerusalem today. The number of Christians in Jerusalem started diminishing during Ottoman times but stabilized during the British Mandate. It continued to decline sharply after the State of Israel was established in 1948 and then again after Israel's occupation of East Jerusalem and annexation of that part of the city in 1967. The number of Christians continues to decline. Many factors contribute to this decline, but a major factor is the official polices of the Israeli authorities toward the Palestinian Arab residents of the city.

Most of Jerusalem's Christian Palestinians were expelled from West Jerusalem during the War of 1948 along with many Muslim Palestinians too, leaving behind them beautiful neighborhoods in the city. These neighborhoods include Talbieh, Baqa and Qatamon, where the elegant villas of many wealthier Christian families were built. Their homes and belongings were seized by the Israeli authorities. Many of these refugees took refuge in the Old City, thus doubling the number of Christians there. During Jordanian rule, from 1948 to 1967, some Jerusalemites moved to Amman because the Jordanians developed the capital and Jerusalem was relegated to a marginal status. However, in the aftermath of the 1967 War, when the Old City was occupied by the Israeli army, many more Christians left, seeking refuge in neighboring Arab countries and in the countries of the wider Palestinian Diaspora. The following table presents the dramatic transformation of the Christian presence in Jerusalem:

Jerusalem demography			
	Jews	Christians	Muslims
1910	45,000	12,900	12,000
1931	51,000	19,300	19,900
1946	99,300	31,400	33,700
1967	196,800	12,900	58,100
1983	306,300	13,700	108,500
2012	497,000	9,000	250,000

The State of Israel annexed East Jerusalem after the 1967 War, separating it from the rest of the West Bank, also occupied during that war. However, the authorities annexed the land of East Jerusalem but did not annex the Palestinians living there.

35

More than 14,000 Palestinian Jerusalemites, Muslims and Christians, absent on the day of the occupation, lost their residency in Jerusalem and therefore they, defined as absentees, and their descendants have been denied the right to live in their city. The Palestinian Jerusalemites who remained were granted the status of permanent residents in Israel by the Israeli authorities, a legal status that left them, as well as their descendants, vulnerable to losing their residency in their own city. This is primarily due to the functioning of the "Entry into Israel" law. This law's regulations specify that permanent residents shall lose their status should they: leave Israel for a period of seven years; acquire permanent residency outside Israel; and acquire foreign citizenship. Recently an amendment has been introduced whereby residence can also be annulled due to "lack of loyalty" to the State of Israel.

Among the hardships faced by Palestinian Jerusalemites, and one of the most recurring, is the issue of family unification. Palestinian Jerusalemites have great difficulty attaining Jerusalem residence rights for their spouses, often from the West Bank, and for their children. Over the past two decades, this situation has caused great uncertainty and suffering for hundreds of families in Jerusalem after the Israeli government suspended family unification applications for Palestinians and applied more strictly the Citizenship and Entry into Israel Law.

Between the years 2003 and 2013, 12,284 applications were made. Of these, 5,629 applications were approved, and 4,249 applications were rejected. Between 2013 and the end of July 2017, 2,666 family unification applications were made. And of this number, 1,246 applications were approved while 600 applications were rejected. The remainder were either suspended or remain pending.

Added to this the problem families face in registering their children in the Israeli population registry. It is a problem because it leaves many babies and children vulnerable because they are without proper medical care or education, not to mention the fact that they officially do not exist. Between 2004 and 2013, 17,616 child registration applications were made. Of this number, 12,247 applications were approved, and 3,933 applications were rejected for different reasons. Between 2013 and the end of July 2017, 8,304 child registration applications were made. And of this number, 5,735 applications were approved with 850 applications rejected. The rest were either suspended or remain pending.

Palestinian Jerusalemites also face a severe housing problem. Over the past two decades, Palestinians have built "illegally," according to the Israeli Planning and Building law of 1965. The surge in "illegal building" was due to the fact that the Israeli authorities did not properly plan for the Palestinian sector. According to the United Nations Office for the Coordination of Humanitarian Affairs (OCHA), "at least a third of all Palestinian homes in East Jerusalem lack an Israeli-issued building permit, potentially placing over 100,000 residents at risk of displacement." Millions of shekels in fines have been collected by the Israeli authorities from Palestinians. Currently, the number of building permits that are granted to Palestinians in East Jerusalem is increasing. However, Palestinian Jerusalemites are facing a new challenge in the high cost of housing units, which on average cost around $400,000 USD per unit. If they decide not to buy a home, the rent they have to pay monthly is exorbitant.

Although Palestinian Jerusalemites pay high taxes like residents in West Jerusalem, there is blatant discrimination in public services when compared to those provided in the west of the city. Among the most important services is education. Education in East Jerusalem is in crisis. According to the Israeli association, Ir-amim, the shortage of classrooms in East Jerusalem was 2,557 for the academic year of 2016/2017. This, coupled with the bad state of the government schools in East Jerusalem, is leading to a considerable number of young people dropping out of school at an early age. According to Ir-amim, the dropout rate in East Jerusalem stands at 33%, the highest dropout rate among all localities in Israel. Many Palestinian youth in Jerusalem join an unskilled labor force providing cheap labor to many Israeli economic enterprises.

Christian Palestinian Jerusalemites are disciples of Jesus Christ and members of the Mother Church, from whose midst witnesses were sent out to preach the good news to the ends of the earth. They are rooted in the Holy City, bringing together in their person a wide array of cultures. Many are those who came to the city as conquerors, visitors, merchants and pilgrims. And yet, the members of the Christian community have remained rooted here, dwelling in the city in times of plenty and want, thriving or merely surviving for 2,000 years.

Christian Jerusalemites are intimately connected to the peoples of the Middle East and strongly linked to the Christian communities in the modern countries of Syria, Lebanon, Jordan and Egypt. Undoubtedly the centuries of history have brought about political, social and cultural challenges that impact their identity. However, today, Christian Palestinians in Jerusalem feel their sense of belonging to the city first and foremost – of being Jerusalemites. Although many might underline their Christian identity before their Arab identity, they strongly identify as Palestinians, the indigenous people of the land and are infused with a particular Christian heritage, as well as with the multiple heritages of the city. Because of the ongoing conflict and enduring instability, some might indeed find it easier to identify with the more powerful and seek closer contacts with the present Jewish Israeli establishment. However, the vast majority of Christian Jerusalemite Palestinians affirm their national belonging to the Palestinian people.

The community is strongly identified with the structures of family and proudly maintained institutions, such as parishes, schools, hospitals and others that serve the welfare of the community. Many Christians are educated in Christian schools and at Christian universities (Bethlehem University and other Christian colleges in the Bethlehem area) and employed within Christian institutions (including a vast array of services for pilgrims). It is important though to underline that these institutions are open to one and all regardless of religious affiliation. Although the Churches have maintained a traditional role, mainly abstaining from involvement in the largely unstable political situation and in the struggles outside of church walls, Churches have contributed greatly to maintaining the Christians in Jerusalem, providing education, housing, employment, health care and social welfare.

A wide array of Christian social associations and movements, scout groups, youth groups, women's groups and other support groups, keep the Christians closely connected to each other. These associations and movements generally transcend the particular denominational identities of the community. Whereas Orthodox, Catholics and Protestants might worship each in his or her own parish, the institutions and associations bring Christians together. Within these structures, Christians are formed, meet one another, marriages are celebrated, and leadership is passed down to the next generation. As a result of these structures, the Christian community, despite denominational fragmentation, appears united, espousing both civic and social values and a high degree of communal solidarity.

However, the future of the community is clouded by the bleak general atmosphere, which includes political instability, shadows of occupation and discrimination, insecurity, and the lack of any prospect for justice and peace. Some members of the community think about leaving by migrating to countries where life would seem simpler. Their hope of a better future often goes no further than dreaming of a place in which there is security, wellbeing and equality for all. Others are focusing on trying to be materially successful and guarantee some kind of normalcy for their families. Jerusalem is sequestered from its most natural space, as it is cut off more and more from the surrounding towns of Bethlehem and Ramallah and their surroundings. The separation barrier that the Israeli authorities have constructed is an obstacle not only to economic, social and cultural development but also to family relationships as it impedes freedom of movement. Isolated from its natural markets, East Jerusalem has been suffocated economically as well. Palestinians, Christians and Muslims find it difficult to plan a future.

Many Christian Jerusalemites cultivate an awareness that they are the custodians of the Holy Places. Their living faith and Christian witness must survive and flower if the Mother Church of all Christians is to be more than a museum. Christian Jerusalemites sense a responsibility to remain steadfast in Jerusalem despite all the woes. Their identity and mission are often founded on simply surviving and remaining in the city – as Christians, as Palestinians and as Arabs. Among themselves, they engage in much debate about possible political strategies. Most Christian Jerusalemites dream of an open city with international guarantees that would ensure freedom of access, freedom of worship and freedom for all those who see Jerusalem as their home. Others, who see this as an unlikely outcome to the conflict, would prefer to see East Jerusalem become the capital of the State of Palestine, a state they have fought for and promote as secular and democratic. There are also those who prefer staying under Israeli rule, having despaired of other possible outcomes of the present situation, preferring the financial and social benefits offered by a rich and powerful system.

For those who are poor or underprivileged, it is difficult to stay in the city. According to official statistics from May 2017, the Israeli National Insurance Institute found that 76% of adults and 83.4% of children in the Palestinian population in East Jerusalem lived under the poverty line. Among these, some Christians are fortunate to receive Church institutional support aside from social welfare from the Israeli system. Young couples often have to leave the city to find housing elsewhere, often in Palestine or in Bethlehem and its surrounding areas, for example. There they are threatened with the loss of their Jerusalem residency, a process that makes them foreigners in the city of their ancestors.

Despite the aid offered by the Churches, many Christians complain that the Church hierarchy and clergy are far removed from the day to day struggles of the people. They sense that the pastors do not share in the everyday life of the people, living in Church institutions, often behind high walls. They expect more of their pastors than aid in employment, housing and education. Whereas Christians do receive support, sometimes rendering them dependent and unable or unwilling to take up responsibility, it is also true that much of the Church hierarchy and clergy provides little leadership in facing the challenges of the socio-political reality. While this might differ from denomination to denomination, it is still true that many members of the Church hierarchy are expatriates.

Beset by many challenges, finding housing and employment, living in insecurity, dealing with occupation and discrimination and facing a variety of hard measures that include loss of residency rights, inability to unite families under one roof, impediments on freedom of movement and heavy taxation, Christian Jerusalemites do have a common sentiment. They are proud to be residents in the Holy City. They also have a common dream: to live in equality and peace in a Jerusalem that is shared by all who live there.

5. West Bank Christians

The West Bank (of the Jordan River) comprises the central hilly ridge of Palestine, plus the Jordan valley. Like Gaza, it remained under Arab control after the Arab Israeli War of 1948 and was then formally annexed to the Kingdom of Jordan. These two regions were militarily occupied by Israel in 1967. The main Palestinian towns of the West Bank are: in the south, Hebron and the traditionally Christian triangle of Bethlehem, Beit Jala and Beit Sahour; in the north, Nablus and Jenin; in the center Jerusalem and Ramallah, which serves as the provisional capital for the Palestinian Authority. The previous section describes the situation in Jerusalem.

Christian Presence

In the West Bank, out of the 3 million Palestinian inhabitants, only about 50,000 are Christian. Almost 10,000 of these live in Jerusalem. The expatriate Christian presence, which is mainly religious men and women, is important in Jerusalem and Bethlehem but almost non-existent in the other regions. The Bethlehem area (Bethlehem, Beit Sahour and Beit Jala) has

45

almost 25,000 Christians. Ramallah has slightly over 10,000 Christians, and in the north (Nablus, Jenin), there are about 5,000 Christians. The majority live in Zababdeh, a large Christian village with 3,000 Christians out of its 4,000 inhabitants. In the region of Nablus-Jenin, several very small communities of Christians live in villages with no more than one hundred people in each village. Some of these villages are reduced to just a few families. These villages were more prosperous in the past, but due to the reduced number of residents and their isolation from other Christian communities, many abandoned their villages and joined bigger communities elsewhere. In Nablus, an important city of more than 250,000 inhabitants, Christians number only 800 people. Jenin, another large city in the north, has only a few dozen Christians living there.

In the West Bank, Christians belong to various denominations: Catholics (Roman, Greek, Maronite), Orthodox, Oriental (Armenian, Syrian, Copt) Anglicans, Lutherans and Evangelicals; in addition to a number of recently founded evangelical communities. All these live side by side in the same town or village. Typically, in every city or village there is a parish, and often more than one, according to the denominations present. Religious services are regularly held in all towns and villages. Often, the church is built in the center of the town or village, surrounded by a parish hall and school, as well as some basic medical services. There are Christian hospitals in Nablus, Bethlehem and Beit Jala. In the Bethlehem area, there are more than 15 private Christian schools alongside the government schools. Higher education is offered at Bethlehem University (Catholic), Dar Al-Kalima College (Lutheran), Bethlehem Bible College (Evangelical) and the Latin Patriarchal Seminary, where Catholic clergy are educated. There is also a Christian founded private university in Bir Zeit. All these institutions, except the Beit Jala Seminary, are attended by Christians and non-Christians.

Impact of the Israeli Occupation

The life of Christian Palestinians in the West Bank is inevitably deeply marked by the consequences of the ongoing Israeli occupation. The Israeli Occupation of the West Bank, which began in 1967, continues today. In 1993 a political change occurred as a result of the Oslo Agreement, which marked the establishment of the Palestinian Authority in Gaza and the West Bank. At the same time, the West Bank was divided in to three zones: zone A, where, in principle, the civil administration and security were entrusted to the Palestinian Authority; zone B, where the civil administration was entrusted to the Palestinian Authority but the security remained under Israeli control; zone C, where the civil administration remains under Israeli civil and security control. In fact, the Palestinian Authority remains totally dependent on Israel, and the Israeli security forces enter and act in all three zones as they see fit.

A major threat to the Palestinian presence in the West Bank is the creeping Israeli appropriation of land through the building of roads and settlements, as well as the expropriation of land for purportedly military purposes. This land is often then transferred for civil settlements. This creeping annexation strangles the life of the Palestinians with a system of military roadblocks and checkpoints, which render free circulation between the various Palestinian localities almost impossible and paralyzes economic and social development. The building of a separation wall between Palestinian and Israeli areas has created new problems. These include cutting off the West Bank from Jerusalem, which constitutes the vital center of Palestinian social and economic life. It also makes access to Jerusalem schools and hospitals almost impossible. This area is also the center of religious life because Muslim and Christian Holy Places are situated there. The West Bank has no air traffic and all the border crossings are under exclusive Israeli control. Israel also collects taxes and custom duties on Palestinian goods and services that should be regularly transferred to the Palestinian Authority. However, Israel often blocks these repayments as a means of exercising pressure on the Palestinian Authority to conform to Israel's priorities.

Christians in Palestinian Society

In this context, Christian Palestinians are an integral part of society. They face the same difficulties and foster the same expectations as all other Palestinians. However, because of their small numbers, Christian Palestinians often strongly feel the negative effects of the ongoing occupation with its manifold limitations on freedom of movement, economic development and job opportunities. In fact, in the West Bank today there is high unemployment, not enough housing, weak enforcement of law and order, a high cost of living and undeveloped infrastructure, including health care and social welfare. Christians tend to be highly educated and thus have high expectations for themselves and their children. These, expectations are often frustrated by the situation. This leads many to contemplate emigration, and some do in fact leave their homeland, never to return.

Christians constitute a small numerical minority of 1% to 2% of the population. This sometimes creates among Christians a feeling of being weak, marginalized and vulnerable. It also fosters fear for the present and future. Some complain of being under-represented and abandoned in society, as they are not given adequate responsibilities and job opportunities in the administration. Others feel a sense of powerlessness in defending themselves when disputes arise with neighbors (for example, disputes regarding property rights), or when they confront criminality in society. Some tend to try and withdraw from general society into a fortress constituted by their religious communities. This leads to a weakening of their sense of belonging to the wider Palestinian society. Recent developments in the broader Arab and Muslim world have strengthened these tendencies of alienation and withdrawal as radical Islamic forces have tightened their grip and imposed new ways of defining the identity of the region. However, the Church encourages Christians to take up their role as part and parcel of the Palestinian people by engaging actively in public life and committing themselves to take an active part in the building of the Palestinian state, in which Christians too must find their place.

Muslim-Christian Relations

Muslim-Christian relations are extremely important. Palestinian society is a mixed society, and the Christian presence is part and parcel of it. Muslims and Christians live together in the same cities and villages and have a common history and culture. They constitute one people. Relations at the level of higher civil and religious authorities are traditionally positive. The Palestinian leadership insist on the importance of the Christian presence, both for the diversity within Palestinian life and society, as well as for contact with the outside world. Late President Yasser Arafat took many measures to consolidate the Christian presence. Easter and Christmas were declared national holidays. In towns or villages with a significant Christian presence, the mayor was to be a Christian. The Palestinian Legislative Council, following the Jordanian model, provides a Christian quota in order to guarantee Christian representatives from every region where Christians live. This quota consists of two representatives from Bethlehem, two from Jerusalem and two from Ramallah. Among the ministers, there are habitually one or two Christians. Christian religious education has the same status as Muslim education, and the Ministry of Education publishes textbooks for both. The Christian books are composed by an ecumenical committee, representing all the various Churches.

In daily life, a pattern of living together has matured over the centuries and has led to good neighborly relations between Christians and Muslims. However, in times of crisis or when quarrels emerge between neighbors, the religious component of identity too often emerges as a dominant one, and the conflict is often aggravated by religious polemics and prejudice. As part of the historical pattern of coexistence, specific structures of mediation that bring together Muslims and Christians personalities have been created spontaneously.

Often, they are called upon to mediate in situations of conflict, particularly if there has been serious injury, damage to property or bloodshed.

The rise of Islamic radicalism with the establishment of extremist political parties is a new phenomenon throughout the Middle East. These developments have influenced mentalities in Palestine too, especially among the youth, and have nurtured aggressive behavior towards non-Muslims. As a reaction, some sectarian tendencies have also emerged among Christians, affirming Christian identity and spreading contempt for non-Christians. Church leaders and those in positions of responsibility reaffirm that religious extremism is not the right way to combat religious extremism.

A central concern among Christians is their decreasing proportion in Palestinian society. Cities like Bethlehem and Ramallah that were overwhelmingly Christian in 1948 have a large Muslim majority today. This demographic change was primarily caused by the influx of Palestinian refugees who fled the State of Israel, many of whom settled in refugee camps and neighborhoods of the West Bank cities. However, two ongoing factors have contributed to an ongoing decrease in the proportion of Christians. First, Christians tend to have smaller families than their Muslim neighbors. Second, many Christians, especially the best educated, have chosen to leave the region in search of a better future.

The phenomenon of emigration is an important factor in the life of the Christians in the West Bank and elsewhere in Palestine. Of course, emigration is not limited to Christians. All people emigrate, fleeing the frustrations and fears spawned by the conflict between Jews, Muslims and Christians, Israelis and Palestinians. However, Christian emigration is proportionally higher than other communities, and Christians, already few in number, are impacted even more than other communities. Indeed, those who emigrate are often the young and the best educated.

A Shared Responsibility

The well-being and future of the Christian presence in Palestine is the responsibility of one and all, Muslims and Christians alike. Together they must work for an open and respectful society, where all enjoy equal rights and bear equal responsibilities. However, remaining rooted in their historical homeland is also a specific Christian task and vocation. The Church was born here, and a vibrant Christian presence must be a constant witness to those roots. As citizens, Christians are called to collaborate in the common struggle for a future of justice and peace, as well as in building an open and law-abiding society. In this society, Christians are a living witness to the Gospel of love, nonviolence and service of others. The building of the future State of Palestine is a unique opportunity where everyone can and should contribute – men and women, Muslims and Christians, believers and non-believers – in order to create a human society where the great richness that results from this diversity constitutes the real beauty of living together in mutual acceptance.

6. Gaza Christians

Of the Palestinians living in Palestine (West Bank including East Jerusalem and Gaza Strip) today, 39% are in Gaza, which constitutes 15% of all Palestinians worldwide. However, it is important to remember that the population of Gaza Strip in 1948 was between 60,000 and 80,000, and it quadrupled almost overnight. By January 1949, there were about 280,000 people in the Strip, the vast majority of these were refugees. Today, there are close to 2 million Palestinians that call the crowded Gaza Strip their home. This is an area that does not exceed 365 sq. km., making it one of the most densely populated locations on the face of the earth. A formal household survey conducted by the YMCA-Gaza, published in May 2014, put the number of Christians at 1,313. Today, that figure is estimated to be less than 1,000 people.

Among the Christians in Gaza, the largest denomination is Greek Orthodox (89%). The Greek Orthodox Church is represented by a Bishop, who resides in the convent alongside the 1,600-year-old Saint Porphyry Church. A smaller Roman

Catholic (Latin) community (8.9%) is served by two priests, who reside in the complex of the Holy Family Church in the Zeitoun neighborhood. There is also an Anglican church in the complex of the Ahli Arab Hospital. A Baptist congregation has sprung up and attracts some Christians to its ranks. Despite the very small number of Christians, Christian institutions are diverse and provide services that are disproportionate to the size of its population.

There are five Christian schools in Gaza providing a co-educational setting of quality education to approximately 3,000 students, among whom are 180 Christians and the remainder are Muslim. Three of the schools are led by the Latin Rite of the Roman Catholic Church. Two of these are administered by the Latin Patriarchate of Jerusalem and one by the Sisters of the Rosary. One of the five Christian schools in Gaza is Greek Orthodox. The fifth school is Evangelical. In the health sector, the Anglican Ahli Arab Hospital, three clinics of the Near East Council of Churches and the Catholic Caritas clinic provide quality medical services to tens of thousands of Gazans on an annual basis. More recently, St. John's Ophthalmic Hospital in Jerusalem has opened a local branch in Gaza City. In addition, the Near East Council of Churches operates four vocational training centers which offer technical training to hundreds every year. The vocational training centers also implement a variety of community development and employment projects. The Greek Orthodox Myrrh Bearers Society offers a variety of programs to aid the community. The Young Men's Christian Association (YMCA), with its 500 strong members, provides sports, cultural, educational and social activities in an atmosphere of respect and tolerance. Finally, the Missionaries of Charity (of Mother Teresa of Calcutta) operate a residential facility for physically challenged and abandoned children, as well as for the elderly. These institutions are constantly looking for ways to better serve the wider community and are eager to contribute to the welfare of society.

Gaza was occupied by Israel in 1967, ending Egyptian control of the Strip. The Palestinian Authority began administration of Gaza after the signing of the Oslo agreements in 1994. The Strip was relatively calm in the following years despite the continued presence of the Israeli occupation authorities in parts of the territory. In 2005, Israel, under Prime Minister Ariel Sharon, unilaterally withdrew from the Gaza Strip after completing construction of a separation wall. In 2006, Hamas, the Islamic Resistance Movement, won the elections to the legislative council in a landslide victory and formed a national government. That same year, Israeli soldier Gilad Shalit was kidnapped and held hostage in Gaza. As a result, a blockade was imposed by Israel and the international community. A few months later in 2007, Hamas completely took over the Gaza Strip. It expelled the Fatah leadership in a violent confrontation and formed a separate Hamas government in the Gaza Strip that continues to hold power.

Since then, Islamic rule has been imposed, making life uncomfortable for many, including Christian individuals and their institutions. The situation deteriorated even further as a result of three successive wars waged against Gaza in the short span of five years. The first began in December 2008, lasting about 20 days. It left behind devastating destruction, much of which remains today. The second was launched in November 2012 and lasted eight days, creating further destruction. The third, and most recent war on Gaza, began in July 2014 and lasted 51 days. This war was the most destructive of all. It resulted in the death of 2,131 Palestinians and injured 11,231 people, including 3,436 children, 3,540 women and 418 elderly. Five-hundred-thousand people were displaced. The destruction was significant: 18,000 housing units were destroyed; an additional 37,650 units sustained serious damage; 62 hospitals and 220 schools were damaged; 22 schools were completely destroyed; 419 businesses were damaged; and 128 businesses sustained complete destruction. After the war, unemployment reached a record high of 70% for youth aged 20-24 and 45% in the total population.

Events in neighboring Egypt, the country that ruled Gaza from 1948 to 1967, have an important influence on the Strip. In recent years, two Egyptian presidents have been toppled. The second of these presidents belonged to the Muslim Brotherhood in Egypt. During his term, favorable relations were fostered with the Hamas leadership in Gaza. However, this ended when he, in turn, was toppled.

All through these years of aggravated crisis, Christian institutions and welfare agencies have come to the rescue, providing emergency financial and moral support in order to alleviate the suffering of the masses in Gaza. This takes the form of providing medicines, medical equipment and covering medical costs and fuel for the institutions working in the health sector. These recipients include the Ahli Arab Hospital, the Near East Council of Churches clinics and the Caritas clinic. Assistance also includes providing cash support, food packages, hygiene packages and clean drinking water. During the hostilities, Christian institutions opened their doors and hearts and converted their premises into temporary shelters to house the countless displaced people and served as distribution centers. Among these institutions are the Greek Orthodox convent and church, the Roman Catholic Holy Family School, the Greek Orthodox Cultural Center and parts of the Ahli Arab Hospital and YMCA. Christian institutions were also at the forefront in rebuilding efforts, including attempting to rebuild homes.

Christian institutions were also able to guarantee a degree of normalcy after the cessation of hostilities as they returned to full functioning immediately. The schools, and in particular the Rosary Sisters School and the Holy Family School, are good examples as they opened for the school year a mere three weeks after the war ended. In response to the reports about the level of trauma sustained by the whole Gaza population, and in particular to the children, a massive psychosocial program of intervention was launched in dozens of schools, kindergartens and health facilities. These interventions reached tens of thousands of people. Such support, during and after the war, has created a respect for Christian institutions among communities in Gaza, especially those directly affected by this outreach. Many Christians in Gaza reported that after the wars, they had been told by their Muslim compatriots how much they appreciated the Christian institutional presence and its service of all.

After the 2014 ceasefire, relative calm was maintained. However, in mid-2018, the situation deteriorated again. With the humanitarian situation on the verge of total collapse, a series of protest events were organized on the border with

Israel to mark the 1948 war. Though most of these mass demonstrations were peaceful and posed no real threat to Israeli soldiers, the Israel army's response was heavy handed. Snipers were placed at the border with orders to shoot and kill any Palestinian who approached the border. The situation climaxed on 14 May 2018, the day the United States moved its embassy from Tel-Aviv to Jerusalem, resulting in the killing of over 60 Palestinians and the injury of over 1,000 in one day. Hospitals were inundated and medical supplies were short. Since then, the situation has remained very tense.

In light of the continuing humanitarian crisis – which includes the near total collapse of water, sewage and electricity networks, as well as the skyrocketing unemployment figures – it is very likely the situation will continue to worsen unless there is a real effort to lift the blockade and allow people to live with dignity.

Despite the strength of Christian institutions and the widespread appreciation of their role, Christians face a myriad of challenges in Gaza. One of the most difficult challenges is trying to live a normal life with the continued blockade imposed by Israel and more recently by Egypt. It is a situation faced by all Palestinians in Gaza. Gaza feels like a very large open-air prison with travel restrictions in full force by both Israel and

Egypt. Youth in particular feel the weight of such travel restrictions as there is a general blanket restriction prohibiting all youth, Christian and Muslim from the age group of 16 to 35, from entering Israel and the West Bank. Even when permits allowing visits to the Holy Places in Bethlehem and Jerusalem for major religious holidays such as Christmas and Easter are issued to Christians in Gaza by the Israelis, youth are mostly excluded.

A second series of challenges for Christian life in Gaza is related to the complications of living under an Islamic regime that seeks to impose Sharia law. Women are expected to conform to Islamic Sharia dress code. In general, freedoms are limited, especially for women. Women studying at universities in Gaza are sometimes asked to leave the class if they are not wearing a veil, Christians included. Alcohol, for example, is prohibited in Gaza, even for the Christians. Christian symbols at Christian schools, including the traditional Christmas tree, are viewed with suspicion. In recent years there has been an attempt to introduce segregation of boys and girls, as well as male and female teachers, in Christian schools also. However, after a rather feeble attempt in 2015 to impose this segregation, the local authorities abandoned the plan after resolute opposition from the Churches in Jerusalem.

The Christians in Gaza represent a small, but active, presence in a region of Palestine that has known much suffering. Christian institutions play a central role in the life of the community, and they provide education, health and social services to all segments of society without discrimination and with Christian values at their core. These Christian institutions were never intended to serve Christians alone. Their attention is focused on serving the marginalized, weak and poor – anyone in need of such services regardless of their background. This open service ensures that Christians are not isolated but integrated into society. These institutions are trusted and respected by all, whether Christian or Muslim. These institutions also play a significant role in interfaith dialogue, lived day in and day out. They are also playing their part in the establishment and development of civil society, where sometimes the Church, through its institutions, is doing the job of governments.

7. Christian Palestinians in Israel

There are about 160,000 Christian citizens of the State of Israel. About three quarters of these Christians are Palestinian Arab citizens of the State of Israel. The others are Christians who have been recognized as related to Jews, and therefore, accepted as part of Jewish society. Recent Israeli Bureau of Statistics reports have noted two interesting facts about the Christian Arab population. First, its people have the lowest birth rate, and second, they have the highest education level when compared with Jewish, Muslim and other communities in the country. The average Christian Palestinian family in Israel had 2.0 children; whereas Jews had 2.4 children, and Muslims had 2.8. Matriculation exams scores of the 66.2% of Christian Palestinian youth who took the exams received scores high enough to enter university. Only 55.1% of Jews and 41% of Muslims who took the exams were high enough to enter university.

Although citizens of the State of Israel have the right to full participation in the political life of the country, all Palestinian

Arab citizens of Israel face multiple levels of discrimination in daily life as non-Jews in a state defined as Jewish and as Palestinian Arabs in the midst of the ongoing Israeli-Palestinian conflict. This discrimination is particularly evident in the development of the community and the resources available for development. It includes housing, education (most importantly access to higher education), employment, health care (most importantly development of health services in Arab locations), municipal services, property rights, etc.

Economically, Christian Arab citizens of Israel are relatively better off than their fellow Christians in Palestine. The state provides many educational, health and welfare services that are not available in Palestine. However, the challenges of ongoing discrimination and difficulty finding jobs, building homes and living an ordinary life encourage many to dream of emigration. In fact, some do succeed in leaving and finding a more promising future in other countries.

Christian Palestinians have always played an important part in the political, cultural and social life of the Palestinian Arab population in Israel. At present (2019), among the Palestinian Arabs serving as representatives of the Arab population in the Israeli parliament (Knesset), there are two Christians. One is on the Joint List, Aida Touma, and the other, Mtanes Shehade, is leader of Balad.

Christian Palestinian Arab citizens of Israel are divided not only according to religious denomination – Greek Catholics, Greek Orthodox, Roman Catholics (Latins), Maronites, Armenians, Copts, Protestants and Evangelicals – but, even more importantly, according to socio-political orientation. In fact, it is true to say that Christian Palestinians in Israel are in a crisis of identity. One can point to four competing areas that vie for allegiance as Christians attempt to formulate their identity relating to the Palestinian, Arab and Israeli components of that identity.

The first constellation emphasizes the Palestinian Arab dimension of identity. Traditionally, denominational allegiance was seen as a source of division, and so overt Christian identification was avoided in order not to underline potential cleavages among Christians and Muslims. Furthermore, identification with Israel is seen as a betrayal of the Palestinian cause because Israel is perceived as responsible for the plight of the Palestinian people. This constellation is prominent among Christians who have been active in political leadership and intellectual life. Such examples include Tawfiq Toubi, Saliba Khamis and Emil Habibi in the Communist Party in the past and

Ramez Jarayseh and others in the present, as well as Azmi Ishara, founder of the National Democratic Alliance.

A second constellation emphasizes Christian identity and often leads to a retreat from political engagement. On the one hand, Christians are frustrated at the Israeli establishment for discriminating against them because they are Palestinian Arabs. On the other hand, they are concerned about the rise of radical Islam in Israel and throughout the region, especially over the past two decades.

A third constellation attempts to maintain a balance between the three primary dimensions of their identity: Christian faith; Palestinian Arab ethnicity; and Israeli citizenship. This complex identity is constantly threatened by Jewish ethno-centricity, by Islamic radicalism and by the continuing Israeli-Palestinian conflict.

Finally, a fourth and still marginal constellation is attempting to formulate a pro-Israeli identity that is rejecting Palestinian and Arab components. The leaders of this current are generally alienated from the traditional Churches. They feel existentially threatened by radical Islam and seek proximity to Israeli power in order to guarantee narrow Christian interests. Some are promoting an Aramean rather than Arab identity. These people support Israeli right-wing political parties and encourage youth to serve in the Israeli army.

Many Christian citizens of Israel, who are exposed to strong Israeli secularism, have a weak link to their churches and faith communities. Nonetheless, the Churches maintain a very important network of schools in Israel that include the top schools in the country. In addition, there are Christian health and welfare institutions that play an important role in the life of the Arab community. In the past, clerics have taken leading roles in the struggle for equality and peace in Israel. An example of this is Greek Catholic Archbishop Yusuf Raya, who spoke out frequently and even went on a hunger strike outside the Knesset in 1973. Another example is Anglican Rev. Shehade, who led the Committee for the Defense of Arab Lands, a part of the Democratic Front for Peace and Equality. Anglican Rev. Riah Abu al-Asal was one of the founders of the Progressive List for Peace. However, Church leadership is not an active participant in the civic life of the country as a whole nor in the life of the Palestinian Arab sector at present.

The approval of the so-called "Nation State Basic Law" by Israel on July 19, 2018 constitutes a new challenge for Palestinian Arab citizens of Israel. The law recognizes Israel as "the historical homeland of the Jewish people," definitely stating that "the right to exercise national self-determination in the State of Israel is unique to the Jewish people." The promulgation of the law was greeted with dismay by all segments of the Palestinian Arab population in Israel. It certainly underlines the need for Christian Palestinian Arabs to seek out their Muslim and Druze compatriots, as well as their Jewish fellow citizens, in the struggle for a society and a state established on the values of justice, peace and equality.

8. Christian Palestinian Diaspora

In 1948, the Palestinian population was 1.2 million in historic Palestine; 8% of which was Christian. During the events of 1947 and 1948 leading to the establishment of the State of Israel, at least 750,000 Palestinians became refugees and 418 Palestinian villages were destroyed. Today, the projected number of Palestinians is close to 12 million worldwide distributed as follows: 38% in Palestine (West Bank including East Jerusalem, and Gaza); 12% in Israel; 44% in the Arab world (mostly in the neighboring countries of Jordan, Lebanon, Syria, and Egypt); and 6% around the world.

Today, a total of 170,000 Christian Palestinians remains in the region, consisting of 50,000 in Palestine and 120,000 in Israel. This makes up less than 17% of all Christian Palestinians worldwide. The remaining 83% of all Christian Palestinians are found outside historical Palestine. The major Christian Palestinian diaspora communities are found in the following countries (the numbers are approximate):

Chile	*350,000*
Honduras	*280,000*
Brazil	*60,000*
USA	*50,000*
Australia	*45,000*
Elsewhere (Arab world, Europe)	*55,000*

The total number of Christian Palestinians, those in the homeland of Palestine and Israel, as well as in the Diaspora, is about 1 million.

Christian Palestinian emigration has gone through three different waves since the late 19th century. The first wave began in the 1880s and lasted until 1940. The second wave spanned the period between 1948 and 1967, which saw the creation of the Palestine refugee problem as a result of the first Arab-Israeli war, the creation of the State of Israel and the 1967 war. This is when Israel occupied the remaining Palestinian territories of the West Bank and Gaza Strip, as well as other Arab lands, such as the Golan Heights and Sinai. The third wave of emigration began in 1967 and continues unabated.

The first wave during the Ottoman period was provoked by the demise of the Empire and was accompanied by sharp economic decline. The extension of military conscription to the Christians in 1909 also contributed to the exodus of young people seeking a better future, particularly in the New World. The successful integration of these Christian Palestinians in the United States, as well as the countries of Latin America, attracted others to follow them. This trend was also strengthened by American missionaries and their activities like the Friends School in Ramallah. The emigrants made a place for themselves in their new countries, and the wealth and influence of Christian Palestinians in countries like Chile and Honduras are particularly notable. Needless to say, assimilation was widespread as the second generation no longer spoke Arabic. Eventually relations with the Palestinian homeland weakened or were even cut off.

The 1948 war resulted in the creation of the Palestine refugee problem when 726,000 Palestinians became refugees, of whom some 50,000 to 60,000 were Christians and some equating to about 10,000 to 12,000 Christian Palestinian families. Entire communities were depopulated of their Christian Palestinian residents. These included Ein Karem, the village of Zachariah, Elizabeth and their son John the Baptist, and the Christian villages on the Lebanese border, Ikrith, Bir'am and Bassa, as well as neighborhoods like Qatamon and Baq'a in Jerusalem. In cities like Jaffa, Lydda, Ramlah and Haifa, only a small remnant of Palestinians remained. Among them were small Christian communities. These refugees became part of the hundreds of thousands of Palestinians hosted in surrounding Arab countries, especially Lebanon and Jordan. Eventually, finding opportunities further afield, they drifted to the Arabian Gulf, Europe and especially the United States, Latin America and Australia. Today a visitor to Chile might be struck by the fact that there are many more Christian Palestinians in Chile than there are in Palestine. A visitor to Sydney or Melbourne, the two largest cities of Australia, might notice that there are more Christian Palestinians from Jerusalem living there than those who remain in Jerusalem. Many have completely assimilated.

Since 1967, the year that Israel occupied East Jerusalem, the West Bank and the Gaza Strip, it is estimated that a number at least equal to the present Christian population in Palestine, 50,000 people, have left because of instability in the political situation, the lack of security and the uninviting economic conditions accompanying continued conflict. In addition to the practical negative effects of an ongoing Israeli occupation, and even when economic prospects improved, many young Christian Palestinian families opt to leave, believing that life in the USA, Australia or elsewhere guarantees a better future for their children. Of course, many Muslims feel the same way. In the Gaza Strip, the emigration of Christians is particularly dramatic due to dire circumstances.

The fact that even relatively well-to-do Christian Palestinian families, particularly young couples in their thirties and forties, decide to leave is an indication of the instability they feel due to the political situation. These young couples usually have professional educations and hold specialized positions, enabling them to have enough resources to think of joining family members abroad. Their argument is basically that current conditions of life, particularly in Palestine (West Bank, Gaza Strip) but also in Israel, are not conducive to the life they would like to live, and more importantly, to guaranteeing their children a secure future. While the political conflict remains unresolved, it serves as a major motivation to leave the homeland. However, increasing emphasis on religious identification, due to the increasing role of religion in the Israel-Palestine conflict, and the concomitant rise of religious extremism and the tensions that it provokes also make many feel insecure.

The various Churches and Christian communities in Palestine and Israel have formally identified the continuing migration of Christian Palestinians from the homeland as a challenge, seeking to stop what is a hemorrhage that threatens the vitality of the Christian witness in the land where Christianity was born. Local Churches are doing much to encourage Christians to stay including providing housing, education, employment and healthcare through the myriad of Christian institutions throughout Palestine and Israel. However, it is clear that the major factor pushing Christians and many others to leave is the Palestinian-Israeli conflict and its devastating effect on the rest of the Middle East over the past seventy years.

In this context, Churches and Christian communities are called to promote among their members an increasing awareness that they have a two-fold vocation in their homeland – one, as citizens and two, as Christians. As citizens, they are called to contribute, together with their Muslim compatriots, to the building of a free and democratic Palestine. As Christians, they are called to continue to bear witness to the Gospel of Christ in the land where it was first preached and lived.

Many Christian Palestinians who opt to emigrate are young educated professionals. Many have relatives abroad and have been able to get foreign passports or residence. Most often the driving force for emigration is concern for the future of children and career prospects. While the Churches cannot provide the answers to all cases of potential emigration, including lack of employment, a recent statistic speaks of the Churches in

Palestine as the second largest employer in Palestine after the Palestinian National Authority. Even though the Churches are not businesses or welfare offices, they can play an important role in the creation of new jobs and employment opportunities. In modern times, the Churches have been at the forefront of education, health and welfare. In Palestine, Church or private Christian institutions of higher learning excel. Examples include the Catholic Bethlehem University, Lutheran Dar Al Kalima and Birzeit University. Likewise, private Christian schools prepare their pupils for a future in their homeland. These institutions, open to both Muslims and Christians, promote education in response to the needs of society and constitute oases promoting a vision of an open society based on equality and civic responsibility.

In facing their many challenges, Christian Palestinians can and should call upon the Diaspora to invest in the homeland. True, Christian Palestinians in the Diaspora manifest political solidarity, especially when dramatic events bring pain, death and injury. Social media is full of messages of solidarity and identification from these Diaspora communities. However, more needs to be done to mobilize these communities, especially the wealthier communities, to get more involved in shaping the future of Palestine. There are various Palestinian sports, cultural, social and religious clubs in Chile, the United

States, Honduras, Brazil, Australia and elsewhere. A more concerted effort should be made to mobilize these associations and individuals to contribute to building an open, egalitarian and free society so that Christian Palestinians, and all other Palestinians too, will remain in their homeland, and those that have left might even consider returning.

9. Christian-Muslim Relations

Stay together, Friends.

Don't scatter and sleep.

Our friendship is made

of staying awake.

- Jalal ad-Din al-Rumi, Muslim mystic (1207-1273)

Today, Christians constitute between 6% to 10% of all Palestinians in the world, however, about 70% of Christian Palestinians live in the Diaspora. In both Palestine and Israel, Christian Palestinians number less than 2% of the total population.

Christian Palestinians are part of a society in which the vast majority of their compatriots are Muslims. Christian and Muslim Palestinians have been living together since the eighth century. They can point to more than thirteen centuries of coexistence. Christian Palestinians, just like Muslims, frequently remember stories told about Muslim women who nursed Christian babies or Christian women who nursed

Muslim babies, especially in the terrible period of the 1948 War. Palestinians have lived, live and will continue to live in one society – frequenting the same schools, working in shared workplaces, buying in the same markets, playing in the same sports fields, celebrating each other's joys and consoling each other in times of loss and grief. Christians and Muslims have fought alongside each other for freedom and have been shot down, imprisoned and exiled together. Christian and Muslim Palestinians have a common history, a common language and a common culture. They belong to the same people. They are called to work together for a common future. The challenge today is not to allow this shared identity and experience to be forgotten, retreating into closed communities where religious difference becomes a reason for separation rather than a celebration of diversity.

Today, Palestinians, whether they be Christian or Muslim, face the same challenges and confront the same difficulties. Palestinians, as one people, struggle for freedom, justice and equality. They dream of independence within secure borders, peace and prosperity. The colonial powers that dominated the Palestinian homeland have always used a policy of "divide and rule" in crushing the dreams of the community to be free. This policy has been continued and strengthened by the State of Israel, whether on Palestinians who became citizens of the

State of Israel in 1948 or on Palestinians who found themselves under Israeli military occupation in 1967. Israel has sought to monopolize all resources in the areas under its control, taking over as much land as possible and weakening Palestinian society as much as possible in order to prevent resistance, or as the saying goes: "more geography, less demography."

An unholy triangle works to break down a sense of being one people so that Palestinian resistance to discrimination and occupation is weakened. This triangle is composed of religious fundamentalist extremism, expansionist Israeli occupation and persisting neo-colonialist racism. Working along the same axes, these forces distort the image of the Palestinian people and their shared political, social, religious, cultural and economic background and traditions. Actions carried out impact the fabric of Palestinian society, create divisions and sow suspicion with regard to national unity and the richness of diversity that characterizes this society. Demoralization breeds helplessness and hopelessness, creating social fragmentation where neighbors take refuge from one another in ghetto-like communities. They adopt a discourse of contempt for one another because of differences in faith, practice and tradition.

In recent years, the entire Middle East has been watching in horror the rise of forces like ISIS (Islamic State in Iraq and Syria) and other extremist groups that sow death and destruction. Their ruthless reign of terror has sought to create uniformity instead of diversity, targeting Muslim dissidents, alternative forms of Islam (Shiites, Alwaites, Druze) and non-Muslims (Christians, Yazidis and others). Their fascination with death and their dream of a uniform, totalitarian society has provoked a nightmare among Christians and other minorities, who have begun to wonder whether there is a future for them in the Middle East.

However, some Christians have realized that there is a seeming convergence of interests between these forces of darkness and the interests of the great powers. The ancestors of today's Christians were suspicious of the colonial powers, who promoted their own interests cloaked in terms like "the protection of Christians" or "encouraging democracy." Christians today should be aware that much is afoot that remains hidden. All Muslims, Christians and other members of society are similarly threatened in both their existence and destiny. Therefore, all must work together to defend a Middle East rooted in diversity and coexistence.

In Palestine-Israel today, Christians must work to enhance the dialogue of shared living, to incarnate our qualitative presence and contextualize, since Christians belong to the land and are an integral part of society. Christian Palestinians have accumulated experience that helps to discern between good and bad government. They are also aware, that in the long run, even a bad local government is better than occupation and discrimination.

Churches and mosques must confront the etiology of hatred, the rejection of the other and intolerance. Religion can and should be promoted as a resource for working for justice, promoting peace and implementing equality. Christian institutions are built upon this vision, and they need to find an even stronger echo in Christian homes and among Christian individuals, starting with the religious leaders of the community. Sermons in churches and mosques can promote these values when delivered to the faithful who gather in the expectation not only of pious sentiments but also leadership, formation and direction. Religious education should encourage critical thinking, as well as deepening the awareness of identity, vocation and mission, making Christians and Muslims proud of their shared history and heritage. Innovation and creativity are not to be feared but embraced in order to prepare for a future beyond occupation and discrimination.

10. Christian-Jewish Relations

Perspectives on Christian-Jewish relations in Palestine must be clearly distinguished from perspectives that are current in Europe and North America. This dialogue has been powered by two strong motors. One is the awakened sense of contrition among Christians with regard to the tragic fate of the Jews in Europe during periods when anti-Judaism and anti-Semitism dominated, culminating in the catastrophe of the Shoah. The other is the embrace of the Biblical and, by extension, the Jewish heritage of the Church. At its center, the fact that Jesus, his disciples and the early Church are part of a Jewish world that has bequeathed to the Church a rich shared heritage, most importantly the Old Testament.

Things look very different from the Palestinian perspective. The reality Palestinians face is one where Jews are less perceived as victims and more identified with the State of Israel and its occupation of Palestinian lands. Furthermore, the Old Testament, because of the way it is exploited by some to justify certain ideologies and policies, arouses concern, particularly with regard to texts about election, promise and land. Many Christians fear fundamentalist exploitation of these texts in the conflict between Palestinians and Israelis.

Yet, Christian Palestinian Arabs, especially those who are citizens of Israel, engage with Jewish Israelis, and one might underline five characteristics of the particular context for Christian-Jewish relations in Israel-Palestine:

1. Non-European, Non-Christian Context
Palestinian society and politics are not predominantly formed by Christian history, culture and tradition. This means that many of the themes and emphases of the predominantly European and North American Jewish-Christian dialogue are not perceived as directly relevant in the West Asian context.

2. The Presence of Islam
Since the seventh century, Islam is the dominant religion in Palestinian society. Thus, for Christians, dialogue with Muslims is a priority. When dialogue with Jews exists at all, it must always take the third partner into consideration; Muslims cannot be ignored. Christian and Muslim Palestinian Arabs, whatever their religious differences might be, live in a common society, speak one language, share one culture and experience one socio-political reality.

3. The reversal of Power Relations

Many contemporary European and North American Christians, profoundly cognizant of their history and context, are sensitive to the marginalized and vulnerable status of Jews in the history of the West. However, Christian Palestinian Arabs reflect on Christian-Jewish relations from the experience of the sovereignty of a powerful Jewish polity. For many Christian Palestinian Arabs, the Jew is often first and foremost a soldier, a policeman or a settler.

4. The Israel-Palestine Conflict as Definitive

From the Western perspective, the watershed in Christian-Jewish relations was the Shoah, which provoked an awakening to a certain teaching of contempt for Jews in Christian circles. From the Christian Palestinian Arab perspective, the establishment of the State of Israel is the critical turning point. The forced displacement of much of the Palestinian population devastated traditional patterns of coexistence among Jews, Muslims and Christians, not only in Palestine, but throughout the Arab world. Henceforth, the question of Palestine is at the center of relations between Christians and Jews in the Holy Land. Furthermore, Christians in the Middle East have expressed explicit concerns that a predominantly spiritual-theological discourse on Jews and Judaism ignores the burning issue of justice and peace and the conflict between Israelis and Arabs. (cf. Kairos Document)

5. The Place of the Bible

The shared Biblical heritage is a fundamental principle in the decades of Christian-Jewish dialogue that has flourished in the past decades in the West. However, the experience of the shared Biblical heritage within the context of Israel-Palestine is not without its ambiguities. The Bible has been used as a foundational text when it comes to establishing a contemporary Jewish claim to the land that Palestinians see as theirs. Zionism, the ideology of Jewish nationalism, often reads the Bible as a legal, historical or even divinely revealed title deed to the land. For many Christian Palestinian Arabs, a major problem is the use of the Bible to dispossess Palestinians of their rights and their land and legitimate expulsion, oppression and discrimination.

In conclusion, there is little dialogue between indigenous Jewish Israelis and Christian Palestinian Arabs because of the political situation. Jewish Israelis and Christian Palestinian Arabs do work together when their political positions coincide. Today in Israel-Palestine, some Jewish Israelis work together with Christian and Muslim Palestinian Arabs in opposing the occupation of Palestinian lands and in fighting discrimination in Israeli society.

86

11. Faith and Charity

Christ said: *"For I was hungry and you gave me something to eat, I was thirsty and you gave me something to drink, I was a stranger and you invited me in, I needed clothes and you clothed me, I was sick and you looked after me, I was in prison and you came to visit me."* When asked by the righteous when did they do this to him, Jesus answered: *"Whatever you did for one of the least of these brothers and sisters of mine, you did for me."* (Matthew 25:35-39) These words present the essence of the Christian message and how it perceives the marginalized, the poor and the needy as brothers and sisters. Charity is deeply rooted within Christian faith. Charity is the act of love, inspired by God's grace bestowed upon us and to mankind. It is not a choice, but rather an essential pillar of our faith; especially as Christians view possessions as an endowment from God, thus in essence all these material goods belong to Him. All that is given by a human person in charity is a response to God's love.

Charity is not an optional matter for Christians. It is an obligation best described in the words of Saint Paul in his First

Epistle to the Corinthians: *"If I speak in the tongues of men or of angels, but do not have charity, I am only a resounding gong or a clanging cymbal. If I have the gift of prophecy and can fathom all mysteries and all knowledge, and if I have a faith that can move mountains but do not have charity, I am nothing. If I give all my possessions to the poor and give over my body to hardship that I may boast, but do not have charity, I gain nothing."* (13:1-3) He then adds: *"and now these three remain: faith, hope and charity. But the greatest of these is charity."* (13: 13)

As is true in every place, in Palestine the Church is not just a building or a clerical hierarchy, but rather a body of believers, living as a community, in the same area, worshiping together and acting in unison. In the history of Palestine, the socio-religious fabric of the community has been repeatedly violated due to violence and instability, the consequences of repeated wars, discrimination, occupation, the general lack of security and absence of governmental support and services. During the war of 1948, many of the most vibrant Christian Palestinian centers were either destroyed or severely damaged, forcing their inhabitants into the Diaspora. Such cities included West Jerusalem, Acre, Haifa, Tiberias, Safed, Nazareth, Jaffa, Lydda, and Ramleh, as well as many villages with large and important Christian communities throughout the country and especially in

Galilee. This severely altered the Palestinian fabric of society. It also meant the Church, in a very short period of time, found itself stripped of its community of believers and activities. Gone were so many Christians as along with their traditions that had enriched the Church and the community alike.

In 1967, yet another disastrous war added to the suffering of the people. Although fewer Palestinians fled their homes, harsh military occupation was imposed, and life in the Occupied Territories became subject to a myriad of laws and rules that had as one of their aims impeding the development of society.

The succession of wars since 1948, the regime of discrimination and the imposition of military occupation has led to an ever-increasing segment of the society in Palestine, including Palestinian Christians, relying on assistance. The Churches and the Christian faithful have often been at the forefront of those extending a helping hand to the needy. In fact, Churches and Christians have always played, and continue to play, a pivotal role in reaching out to those in need, serving one and all, Christian and non-Christian, with respect and dignity. Churches, working hand in hand with the community of believers and Christian aid organizations from overseas, share in the efforts to reach out to the needy, especially those in the margins, the weakest members of society.

In Palestine today, the Church and Christians provide a vastly disproportionate part of the services needed by the entire population. In certain areas, where the political, socio-economic foundations of a community have been destroyed, the Church, her institutions, believers and supporters, sometimes standalone facing the daunting task of providing relief, a minimal degree of normality and the hope of rebuilding. Despite the Church's limited finances and other resources, Church institutions have ensured shelter, food, healthcare, education, employment and other forms of welfare for many of the region's refugees, poor and handicapped through the decades. This continues today as disaster strikes surrounding countries in the Middle East, Syria, Iraq and elsewhere. Providing for such needs touches upon fulfilling basic human rights, and it is the state's responsibility to make them available. In the absence of a competent state, it falls upon the Church and church-related organizations to fill this ever-widening gap.

Charity is not only the act of giving but also of organizing and mobilizing the community so that charity also empowers and accompanies those who enjoy its benefits. This allows those who benefit from charity to become givers themselves. Suitable organization of the community reduces the burden on the

Church It enables both a sharing of responsibility and an engagement of one and all in the pastoral outreach.

The Church in Palestine attempts to work hand in hand with the community of faithful by undertaking the following steps, which are necessary to effectively face the challenge:

• Instill a sense of charity at an early age. While not all attend Mass, the majority of children attend Christian schools in the Holy Land. This is where the formation starts, especially during religion classes. A guided curriculum and a well-studied approach are assets to both teachers and students.

• Clubs, such as the Scouts, are another focus group. Charity work is an integral part of regular activities, such as visits to those who are isolated in hospital, in orphanages or other institutions. Such initiatives also serve as a meeting place for young adults to interact and socialize, exchange ideas and share experiences.

• Homilies in church are used to convey a direct message to the parishioners, highlighting and emphasizing the importance of charity as part of Christian faith and underlining how much the Church needs the community's involvement and direct input.

• Parish priests organize specific activities and encourage parishioners to join in the implementation of the initiatives set forth by the Church and Christian institutions, in the hope that the community becomes engaged and adopts such initiatives, developing programs of its own.

- Christians are visited annually during Epiphany season for the blessing of homes. Parish priests not only carry the message of charity and love of one another to each household, but they also have the occasion to assess their faithful's socio-economic status, their potential and their needs.

- Campaigns that encourage Christians to give during seasons like Christmas and Lent are a part of Church life. The marginalized, poor, secluded, as well as the elderly and handicapped, should be kept in mind all year.

- Social media is used as an effective and potent tool to make the community conscious of the merits of charity and encourage social activism. Coverage of initiatives that exhibit generosity and show volunteerism with the needy encourages others to become involved.

- There is a constant need to reorganize existing charitable organizations and societies, launching them anew with vision and mission statements. This move attracts the involvement of the younger generation, infusing veteran programs and projects with new ideas.

Charity is not only the act of almsgiving and one does not need to be wealthy to contribute. Each one has something to give.

Some have money. Others have time, energy, patience and the ability to listen. Still others have talents. Christian Palestinians are constantly challenged to share with those less fortunate, not only from within the Christian community but also with those outside of it. It is not possible to restrict one's faith to attending church once a week. The Christian faith demands a profession of love of neighbor that finds its expression in the work done with those most in need. If Jesus were to ask Christian Palestinians today, *"What did you do for the least of these brothers and sisters of mine?"*, they would have much to answer. They would point to actions in Palestinian refugee camps and Bedouin villages work among those whose homes have been destroyed and whose lands have been confiscated, and support of those whose family members have been killed or imprisoned. Not all charitable people are Christians in Palestine today, but to be a true Christian, one must be charitable.

12. The Future

General Situation

In the prevailing geopolitical situation, many voices are heard today denouncing the sufferings and persecutions of Christians in the Middle East. Some even proclaim that, very soon, there will be no Christians left in that region. Others try rather to see what can be done to preserve and consolidate their presence. Christians living in Israel-Palestine share in this general tension and uncertainty, but they have also their own specific challenges to face. These are a consequence of the lack of a solution to the Israeli-Palestinian conflict, one of the main sources of instability in the region.

The future of the Christian presence in Israel-Palestine, as well as throughout the Middle East, is inseparable from this context. Christians are part and parcel of the countries where they are rooted and live out their lives as they have for the past two thousand years. They are part and parcel of the peoples with whom they share the same history and the same culture.

Given the general instability that is the consequence of the many rapid and radical changes that have taken place in the region over the past years, it is impossible to foresee what the future holds. The same is true for the Christian presence. In fact, it is less important to predict the future than to reflect on the primary needs of the present and on what should be done so that a Christian future may indeed be possible.

Emigration

The emigration of Christians is perhaps the most concrete consequence of the prevailing situation and is often mentioned as the main threat to their future presence. It raises vital questions, and therefore needs to be studied in a systematic way. Do we have exact numbers of those who are leaving? Which sectors of human society and of the Christian communities are most affected by it? What are the underlying reasons? What are the foreseeable consequences? What can and what should be done to slow down the emigration trend?

The causes of the emigration of Christians are manifold, political, social, and economic in nature. In Palestine, the ongoing Israeli occupation, with the lack of political freedom, the violation of basic human rights and the many restrictions on movement of persons and goods within Palestine as well as across the borders, render normal economic and social development impossible. As a consequence, many Palestinians tend to look to the West for a better future, above all for their children. Because of their small numbers, Christians are at times more affected by this abnormal situation. They tend to emigrate between twice and three times more in proportion to Muslims. Christian families are generally also smaller in size, and Muslims receive more support from the extended family, beyond the nucleus of parents and children. Hence Christians tend to emigrate between two and three times more in proportion to Muslims. Consequently, the danger is that the percentage of Christians in the population diminishes to the point that they become insignificant and can no longer exercise any influence in Palestinian society.

It is mistaken to point to religious persecution of Christians by Muslims, as some Israeli or fundamentalist Evangelical spokespeople do. They use this as a propaganda tool to discredit the Palestinian Authority and to undermine traditional coexistence between Christians and Muslims.

Christian communities and their leaders promote various initiatives in order to slow down emigration. Some of these include providing quality schools, initiating and maintaining housing projects and creating job opportunities. However, this can only be a partial and temporary response. The only real solution to the problem is the end of Israeli occupation of Palestine and the elimination of the various discriminatory measures that affect the life of those defined as "non-Jews" inside Israel.

Participation in Public Life

This political solution extends of course far beyond the control and capabilities of the local Christians. However, at the same time, the future of their presence requires that they collaborate with their fellow citizens in building their society and their future together. They need to rediscover and deepen their belonging to the human society in which they are called to live. They need to strengthen their commitment to an active participation in the various domains of public, economic, cultural and political life. How this could be done requires careful planning by civic and religious authorities. Above all is it necessary to promote the preparation of new leadership. Special programs could be set up to that aim at schools and youth movements.

The pastoral activity of the Churches should also aim to help lay persons discover that this participation in public life is part and parcel of their being Christians. It is their specific vocation in the Church and in society.

Building a United Community that Reaches Out

Building a strong and united community is the basic requirement for any concerted action aiming at promoting the future of the Christian presence in the country. An ongoing collaboration between Church leadership and key lay persons in parishes and Christian institutions should strive to overcome traditional prejudices and divisions within the communities and among the various communities and different confessions. Youth are called to play their unique role, given that they can more easily free themselves from traditional stereotypes and invent new ways to tackle old problems. They should be able to count on the experience and encouragement of the older generation. Since Christians cannot live in isolation, the strong community that all are called to build together must be a community that reaches out to others, who are different in social status and religious conviction.

Interreligious Relations

Participation in public life also requires a reflection on and a preparation for interreligious dialogue and collaboration. In the first place, this must focus on Muslims, but also on Jews. In this domain, Christians do promote the vision of a pluralist society based on the principle of equal citizenship for all. This vision is without distinction based on religion or communitarian belonging and insists on equal rights and duties for one and all.

External Factors

To a large extent, the present geopolitical situation is due to the many political, economic and military interventions of Western powers in the Middle East. Countries as a whole and local populations often have the impression that all decisions concerning their present and future are taken in the West. These decisions are made without consultation with them and without taking into consideration their needs and aspirations. They seek to make their voices heard, and these attempts degenerate at times into violent reactions and anti-western aggression. One cannot justify these acts of violence, but one should try to understand what they seek to communicate to the wider world, discerning the kinds of injustice and frustration that are at their roots. Therefore, it is not enough to put a military end to the extremist acts of violence. One must also take necessary action for repairing the injustices that are at their origin.

The enduring Israeli-Palestinian conflict is also, to a considerable extent, the consequence of a variety of foreign interventions. As a consequence, the international community must assume its responsibility and cooperate effectively in searching for a solution. Furthermore, the relationship of power between Israelis and Palestinians is so imbalanced that the two sides cannot come to a just solution on their own. All efforts to come to an agreement and all implementation of a possible agreement have to be accompanied constantly by the international community.

International Relations

Can the Christians in Israel-Palestine contribute to such a solution, which is of vital importance for the future of their presence in their homeland? They can and do make use of the international relations they have at their disposal to broadcast their message, which is the urgent need for a just and lasting peace, as well as the responsibility of the international community

Christians in the Holy Land have the right to count on the support of their brothers and sisters in Christ worldwide. However, it is up to them to point out that, being Christians, their lives in the present and the future of their presence are inseparable from the wider human society in which they live. Additionally, all help must take into consideration the fullness of their environment. All attempts, conscious or unconscious, that isolate the Christian community from their neighbors and compatriots do more harm than good.

A Call for Personal Commitment

The future of Christians in Israel-Palestine depends on many external factors that are far beyond their own capacities and control, but to a great extent, they also hold their future in their own hands. It is a question of commitment, of faith and of hope. As disciples of Christ, they are called to be living witnesses to the message of equality, liberty, universal fraternity, reconciliation and love for all. This witness demands to be translated into concrete action of service, solidarity and constructive collaboration beyond all barriers of religion, language, nationality and culture.

Section ll: Justice and Peace Commission Statements

Justice and Peace Commission Statements

1. The Present Conflict in the Holy Land

2. Christian Palestinians Are Arabs

3. Are Christians Being Persecuted in the Middle East?

4. Call for a Courageous Change

5. Attempts to Mobilize Christians into the Israeli Military

6. An Attempt to Divide Palestinian Christians

7. Elections in Israel: Voters, Be Responsible and Vote

8. Christmas Message – 2015

9. A New Vision

10. Beyond Occupation: Towards a Common Understanding

11. Prisoners' Hunger Strike

12. The Question of Normalization

13. Defining Terminology

14. On the Demolition of Khan al-Ahmar

15. On the Nation State Law, Passed by the Israeli Knesset

16. Righteousness and Peace Will Kiss Each Other

17. Restoring Property to Original Owners

18. Annex: Statutes of the Justice and Peace Commission

1. The Present Conflict in the Holy Land: The Church's Position

(September 1, 2016)

This text was prepared by some members of the Justice and Peace Commission as a position paper on the situation in the Holy Land. It was commissioned by the Catholic hierarchy. It serves as an introduction here to the other official statements by the Justice and Peace Commission between 2014 and 2018.

1. The Holy Land today is home to two peoples, Israeli and Palestinian, and three religions, Judaism, Christianity and Islam. We believe this diversity is willed by God and should be received as a gift. Saint John Paul II described this land and focused particularly on the Holy City of Jerusalem:

> *"It is a land which we call holy, indeed the land which was the earthly homeland of Christ who walked about it 'preaching the gospel of the kingdom and healing every disease and every infirmity.' (Matt 4:23) (...) Before (Jerusalem) was the city of Jesus the Redeemer, Jerusalem was the historic site of the biblical revelation of God, the meeting place, as it were, of heaven and earth, in which more than in any other place, the word of God was brought to men. Christians honor her with a religious and intent concern because there the words of Christ so often resounded, there the great events of the Redemption were accomplished: the Passion, Death and Resurrection of the Lord. In the city of Jerusalem, the first Christian community sprang up and remained throughout the centuries a continual ecclesial presence despite difficulties.*

> *"Jews ardently love her, and in every age venerate her memory, abundant as she is in many remains and monuments from the time of David, who chose her as the capital, and of Solomon, who built the Temple*

there. Therefore, they turn their minds to her daily, one may say, and point to her as the sign of their nation. Muslims also call Jerusalem 'holy,' with a profound attachment that goes back to the origins of Islam and springs from the fact that they have their many special places of pilgrimage and for more than a thousand years have dwelt there, almost without interruption.

"Besides these exceptional and outstanding testimonies, Jerusalem contains communities of believers full of life, whose presence the peoples of the whole world regard as a sign and a source of hope – especially those who consider the Holy City to be in a certain way their spiritual heritage and a symbol of peace and harmony."
Cf. Pope John Paul II, *Redemptionis Anno* Apostolic Letter (April 20, 1984)

2. The Holy Land has become a land of conflict. This conflict pits two peoples against one another. With the creation of the State of Israel in 1948 on 78% of the territory of historic Palestine, one people, the Israeli Jews, received independence and international recognition. Since then, the other people, the Palestinian Arabs, have remained stateless, under occupation and in exile. The conflict worsened in 1967, when the State of Israel occupied the remaining 22% of historic Palestine and imposed military rule on these areas.

Whereas Jewish Israelis experience full autonomy and international legitimacy within the framework of a national state, Palestinian Arabs live without full equality and face discrimination in Israel. They live under occupation in the areas occupied by the Israeli military in 1967 or live in a far-flung diaspora of refugees – many dreaming of the day they can return home.

3. The Church believes that a solution is possible. It is not, however, the task of the Church to determine the concrete details of the solution. The Church maintains that any legitimate solution needs to ensure:
- Justice for all people in the Holy Land today.
- Equality for all citizens.
- Freedom for all individuals, including complete religious freedom.
- Mutual respect that ensures that all find their place within society.
- Respect for international law.

The Church believes that just as there was a time before the conflict that the peoples of the Holy Land, Jews and Arabs, Muslims, Jews and Christians, lived side by side as neighbors, this is also possible today. The Church also holds that there will come a day, sooner better than later, when justice and peace will be realized, and the conflict will come to an end. This Land is not doomed to conflict, and the Church prays ceaselessly and works tirelessly to promote a discourse and reality of justice and peace, as well as a vision that opens new possibilities on the horizon.

Furthermore, the Church does not believe that the conflict is a religious one. Rather, it is a conflict between two national movements – one of the Jewish Israelis and one of the Palestinian Arabs. Sadly, religion and its texts and symbols are manipulated by the political leadership to promote the conflict and absolutize and radicalize the claims of each side. Unfortunately, certain interpretations of the Bible, both Jewish and Christian, fuel the conflict rather than promote justice and peace.

4. Jerusalem, is the heart of the Holy Land and thus also the heart of the conflict. It is the city made holy in God's plan of salvation for all people. However, it must be recognized as holy for all three religions – Judaism, Christianity and Islam. It is the

patrimony of the faithful of the three religions and the pulsating social, political and cultural center for the Jewish Israeli and Palestinian Arab peoples. According to international law, East Jerusalem is a part of the territories occupied by Israel in the 1967 War. Whatever resolution to the conflict is adopted, complete freedom of access for the faithful of the three religions to Jerusalem and the sovereignty of both peoples in Jerusalem must be respected.

5. The Holy Places of all the faithful in the Holy Land must be protected. The existing status quo, developed over centuries, must be respected. The faithful must be able to visit their shrines, administer them and develop them for the benefit of the entire religious community.

6. Christians are rooted in the people to which they belong. They are not stuck in some middle place but rather have their roots in the language, history, culture and society of their people. Indeed, the vast majority of the Christians in the Holy Land are Palestinian Arabs. Since 1948, there is a growing number of Christians who are part of Israeli Jewish society.

Therefore, the Christians are not a bridge between the two parties to the conflict. They are a leaven within the society to which they belong. They are cultivating a vision of life that is compatible with the Gospel. They are not called to shut themselves off from their compatriots. They are instead encouraged to play an active role in society that promotes a vision of the human person and society that is based upon the values of the Gospel.

Christians do not seek special protection as a minority but rather seek equality and freedom as full members of society. The best way to protect Christians and ensure their future is to exert every effort to bring the conflict to an end, promote justice and equality and work for the prosperity of the entire society.

Christians in the Holy Land express their particular vocation through their many institutions, schools, universities, hospitals, homes for the elderly and the handicapped, etc. These institutions are open to all and serve all. This is a particular Christian way of building the Kingdom of Heaven in the here and now.

7. The Christians in the Holy Land are a people of dialogue by both identity and mission. The 2000 General Pastoral Plan of the Catholic Churches in the Holy Land teaches: "In our Holy Land, this dialogue includes members of the three religions (Islam, Christianity and Judaism), as well as members of other denominations that include Druze, Samaritans, Bahai, etc. We hope that our Holy Land can become a unique and distinguishing place of coming together and of love among the religions, in the service of our societies and the universal service of humanity. Everyone expects this corner of the world to be a source of inspiration because of its spiritual and social grandeur, despite all the obstacles which oppose this dialogue" ("Relations with Believers of Other Religions" Chapter 13 of *The General Pastoral Plan*, Assembly of Catholic Ordinaries in the Holy Land, Jerusalem 2001.)

A dialogue among all Christian communities seeks to promote the unity of the Church and further her mission to bear witness to justice, peace, equality and freedom. The Church also constantly seeks dialogue with Muslims and with Jews, albeit each according to a specific context, in different ways and with different agendas to promote better understanding, mutual respect and a shared mission within society.

8. The Church lives from the Word of God and is constantly nurtured by reading, meditating and praying Holy Scripture. However, at the same time, the Church does not extract quotations from scripture to legitimize or justify particular ideologies or political options. As the Holy See has repeated: "The existence of the State of Israel and its political options

should be envisaged not in a perspective which is in itself religious, but in their reference to the common principles of international law." (*Notes on the correct way to present the Jews and Judaism in preaching and catechesis in the Roman Catholic Church*, Commission for Religious Relations with the Jews, 1985.)

9. In conclusion, the Church is committed to ongoing and tireless prayer, action and advocacy for justice and peace in the Holy Land. The Church is called to be a prophetic voice pointing to a horizon that promises life in abundance for all – Jewish Israelis and Palestinian Arabs, Jews, Muslims and Christians. The Church must carefully form the entire Christian community, bishops, priests, religious and lay people, by following developments on all levels, including in the political situation, so that it can speak out for justice and for equality. The Church is called to be a leaven within society that calls as the voice in the wilderness to make a way for the coming of the Lord. Pope Francis, at the invocation for peace held at the Vatican on June 8, 2014, has reminded us: "*We have heard a summons, and we must respond. It is the summons to break the spiral of hatred and violence, and to break it by one word alone: the word 'brother.' But to be able to utter this word, we have to lift our eyes to heaven and acknowledge one another as children of one Father.*"

2. Christian Palestinians Are Arabs
March 19, 2014

Israeli policy makers are increasingly insisting that Christian Palestinians are not Arabs and not part of the Palestinian people. This has been expressed in the campaign to draft Christian Palestinians into the Israeli military and most recently in a law proposed by Member of Knesset Yariv Levin, which introduces a distinction between Christian and Muslim Palestinians and states that Christian Palestinians are Christians and not Palestinians.

We, the heads of the Catholic Church in Israel, would like to clarify that it is neither the right nor the duty of the Israeli civil authorities to tell us who we are. In fact, most of our faithful in Israel are Palestinian Arabs. They are obviously Christians too. They are also citizens of the State of Israel. We do not see any contradiction in the definition of identity as Christian Palestinian Arabs who are citizens of the State of Israel.

We address our words to all Christian Palestinians, whether in Israel or in Palestine or anywhere they may be in the world. They are, all, wherever they are, Palestinians and Christians and citizens.

Indeed, there are some Christians in Israel, a small, marginal minority, who are supporting this campaign to redefine our identity. We cannot say whether they do so out of self-interest, from fear or for dreams of having full equality. However, we must point out that they cannot pretend to be the spokespeople of all Christian Palestinians in Israel.

The people of this land – Jews, Christians, Muslims and Druze – have lived here for centuries and have known successive governments. Christians, Muslims, Druze and some Jews who have always lived in the land together insist that their shared common identity, which has developed over centuries, is Palestinian.

This campaign clearly has as its aim to divide Christians from their Muslim compatriots. However, it is equally dangerous because it will divide Christians among themselves even further.

If the Knesset indeed seeks the good of the citizens of Israel, it should invest every effort to legislate laws that remove all discrimination against Jews or Arabs, Christians, Muslims or Druze. In creating a society that unites all citizens in equality and strives for justice and peace, there will remain no reason to fear for anybody. Israelis and Palestinians, Christians, Muslims and Druze, can live together in mutual respect and dignity, working together to build a better future.

3. Are Christians Being Persecuted in the Middle East?

April 2, 2014

Persecution! In many parts of the Western world, this word is on people's lips. It is said that Christians are being persecuted in the Middle East today! However, what is really happening? How should we speak in truth and integrity as Christians and as the Church about the suffering and violence going on in the region?

There is no doubt that the recent upheavals in the Middle East, initially called the Arab Spring, have opened the way for extremist groups and forces. They are wreaking havoc in many countries, particularly in Iraq, Egypt and Syria in the name of a political interpretation of Islam. There is no doubt that many of these extremists consider Christians as infidels, as enemies, as agents of hostile foreign powers or simply as an easy target for extortion.

However, in the name of truth, we must point out that Christians are not the only victims of this violence and savagery. Secular Muslims, all those defined as "heretic," "schismatic" or simply "non-conformist," are being attacked and murdered in the prevailing chaos. In areas where Sunni extremists dominate, Shiites are being slaughtered. In areas where Shiite extremists dominate, Sunnis are being killed. Yes, the Christians are at times targeted precisely because they are Christians who have a different set of beliefs and are unprotected. However, they fall victim alongside many others who are suffering and dying in these times of death and destruction. They are driven from their homes alongside many others, and together they become refugees in total destitution.

These uprisings began because the peoples of the Middle East dreamed of a new age of dignity, democracy, freedom and social justice. Dictatorial regimes, which had guaranteed "law and order" but at the terrible price of military and police repression, fell. With their fall, the order they had imposed crumbled. Christians had lived in relative security under these dictatorial regimes. They feared that, if this strong authority disappeared, chaos and extremist groups would take over, seizing power and bringing about violence and persecution. Therefore, some Christians tended to defend these regimes. Loyalty to their faith and concern for the good of their country, should perhaps have led them to speak out much earlier by telling the truth and calling for necessary reforms of more justice and respect of human rights. They would have been standing alongside many courageous Christians and Muslims who did speak out.

We fully understand the fears and sufferings of our brothers and sisters in Christ, when by violence they lose members of their families and are driven out of their homes. They have the right to count on our solidarity and prayers. In certain circumstances their only consolation and hope is to be found in Jesus' words: "Happy are those who are persecuted in the cause of right: theirs is the kingdom of heaven." (Mt 5:10) However, the repetition of the word "persecution" in some circles, usually referring only to what Christians suffer at the hands of criminals claiming to be Muslims, plays into the hands of extremists, at home and abroad. These extremists aim to sow prejudice and hatred, setting peoples and religions against one another.

Christians and Muslims need to stand together against the new forces of extremism and destruction. All Christians and many Muslims are threatened by these forces that seek to create a society devoid of Christians and where only very few Muslims will be at home. All those who seek dignity, democracy, freedom and prosperity are under attack. We must stand together and speak out in truth and freedom.

All of us, Christians and Muslims, must also be aware that the outside world will not make any real move to protect us. International and local political powers seek their own interests. We, alone, can build a common future together. We have to adapt ourselves to our realities, even realities of death, and must learn together how to emerge from persecution and destruction into a new dignified life in our own countries.

Together, we must seek out all those who dream as we do of a society in which Muslims, Christians and Jews are equal citizens, living side by side. Together we must build a society in which new generations can live and prosper.

Finally, we pray for all – for those who join their efforts to ours, and for those who are harming us now or even killing us. We pray that God may allow them to see the goodness He has put in the heart of each one. May God transform every human being from the depth of his or her heart, enabling them to love every human being as God does, He who is the Creator and Lover of all. Our only protection is in our Lord, and like Him, we offer our lives for those who persecute us, as well as for those who stand in defense of love, truth and dignity with us.

4. Call for a Courageous Change
July 8, 2014

"A voice is heard in Ramah, lamentation and bitter weeping. Rachel is weeping for her children; she refuses to be comforted for her children, because they are no more." (Jeremiah 31:15)

A Reality of Violence and Mourning

Israel and Palestine are echoing with the cries of mothers, fathers, brothers, sisters and all loved ones of the young people who have fallen victim to the latest round in the cycle of violence that plagues this land. Some of their faces are well known because the media have covered in detail their lives by interviewing their parents and bringing them alive in our imaginations. Far more numerous are the others who are mere statistics, nameless and faceless. This selective coverage, mourning and memory are themselves part of the cycle of violence.

We offer our sincere condolences to all Israelis and Palestinians in mourning. We must continue to pray that those who have fallen recently will be the last to die violent deaths in this escalation of hatred and vengeance.

A Language that Breeds Violence

"The tongue is a small member, yet it boasts of great exploits. How great a forest is set ablaze by a small fire! And the tongue is a fire. The tongue is placed among our members as a world of iniquity; it stains the whole body, sets on fire the cycle of nature, and is itself set on fire by hell. (...) With it we bless the Lord and Father, and with it we curse those who are made in the likeness of God." (James 3:5-6. 9)

Our hope to bring the cycle of violence to an end is shattered by the irresponsible language of collective punishment and revenge that breeds violence and suffocates the emergence of any alternative. Many in positions of power and political leadership remain entrenched, not only unwilling to enter into any real and meaningful process of dialogue but also pouring oil on the fire with words and acts that nurture the conflict.

The violent language of the street in Israel that calls for vengeance is fed by the attitudes and expressions of a leadership that continues to foster a discriminatory discourse promoting exclusive rights for one group and the occupation with all of its disastrous consequences for the other. Settlements are built. Lands are confiscated. Families are separated. Loved ones are arrested and even assassinated. The occupation leadership seems to believe that the occupation can be victorious by crushing the people's will for freedom and dignity. They seem to believe that their determination will ultimately silence opposition and transform wrong into right.

The violent language of the Palestinian street that calls for vengeance is fed by the attitudes and expressions of those who have despaired of any hope to reach a just solution to the conflict through negotiations. Those who seek to build a totalitarian, monolithic society, in which there is no room for any difference or diversity, gain popular support by exploiting this situation of hopelessness. To these we also say: Violence as a response to violence breeds only more violence.

Breaking Out of the Cycle of Violence
At the invocation for peace in Israel and Palestine, held in the Vatican on June 8, 2014, Pope Francis said: "*Peacemaking calls for courage, much more so than warfare. It calls for the courage to say yes to encounter and no to conflict; yes to dialogue and no to violence; yes to negotiations and no to hostilities; yes to respect for agreements and no to acts of provocation; yes to sincerity and no to duplicity. All of this takes courage; it takes strength and tenacity.*"

We need to recognize that the kidnapping and cold-blooded murder of the three Israeli youth and the brutal vengeance killing of the Palestinian youth are products of the injustice and of the hatred that the occupation fosters in the hearts of those prone to such deeds. These deaths are in no way justifiable, and we mourn with those who mourn the waste of these young lives. It is a tragic exploitation of the tragic death of the three Israelis to exact collective punishment on the Palestinian people as a whole and on its legitimate desire to be free. It also promotes more violence and hatred.

At the same time, we need to recognize that resistance to occupation cannot be equated with terrorism. Resistance to occupation is a legitimate right. Terrorism is part of the problem. Again, we say to one and all: Violence as a response to violence breeds only more violence.

The present situation in Gaza is an illustration of the never-ending cycle of violence in the absence of a vision for an alternative future. Breaking out of the cycle of violence is the duty of all, oppressors and oppressed, victims and victimizers. In order to commit themselves to this aim, all must recognize in the other a brother or sister to be loved and cherished rather than an enemy to be hated and eliminated.

Need for Radical Change
We need radical change. Israelis and Palestinians together need to shake off the negative attitudes of mutual mistrust and hatred. We are called to educate the younger generation in a new spirit that challenges the existing mentalities of oppression and discrimination. We need to shake off any leadership that feeds on the cycle of violence. We must find and support leaders who are determined to work for justice and peace and who recognize that God has planted here three religions – Judaism, Christianity and Islam – and two peoples – Palestinian and Israeli. We must find leaders who are clear-sighted and courageous enough to face the urgency of the present situation. These leaders need to make the difficult decisions that are needed. These leaders must, if necessary, be ready to

sacrifice their political careers for the sake of a just and lasting peace. Such leaders need to have the vocation to be healers, peace makers, seekers of justice and visionaries of the alternatives to the cycle of violence.

We remember the recent visit of Pope Francis to our region and his incessant call for justice and peace. In his meeting with the Palestinian leadership on May 25, 2014, he said: "*In expressing my closeness to those who suffer most from this conflict, I wish to state my heartfelt conviction that the time has come to put an end to this situation which has become increasingly unacceptable. For the good of all, there is a need to intensify efforts and initiatives aimed at creating the conditions for a stable peace based on justice, on the recognition of the rights of every individual and on mutual security. The time has come for everyone to find the courage to be generous and creative in the service of the common good.*" Likewise, in his meeting with the Israeli leadership on May 26, 2014, he said: "*Here I renew my plea that all parties avoid initiatives and actions which contradict their stated determination to reach a true agreement and that they tirelessly work for peace, with decisiveness and tenacity. There is likewise need for a firm rejection of all that is opposed to the cultivation of peace and respectful relations between Jews, Christians and Muslims.*"

Role of Religious Leaders
Our role, as religious leaders, is to speak a prophetic language that reveals the alternatives beyond the cycle of hatred and violence. This language refuses to attribute the status of enemy to any of God's children. It is a language that opens up the possibility of seeing each one as brother or sister. Pope Francis at the invocation for peace cried out: "*We have heard a summons, and we must respond. It is the summons to break the spiral of hatred and violence, and to break it by one word alone, the word 'brother.' But to be able to utter this word we have to lift our eyes to heaven and acknowledge one another as children of one Father.*"

118

Religious leaders are invited to use language responsibly so that it becomes a tool to transform the world from a wilderness of darkness and death into a flourishing garden of life.

"Blessed are those who hunger and thirst for righteousness, for they will be filled.

Blessed are the merciful, for they will receive mercy.

Blessed are the pure in heart, for they will see God.

Blessed are the peacemakers, for they will be called children of God." (Matthew 5:6-9)

5. Attempts to Mobilize Christians into the Israeli Military: The Case of Christian Arab Citizens of Israel

July 14, 2014

Introduction

According to Israeli law, all permanent residents of Israel, male and female, are eligible to be called up to serve in the Israeli military.[3] In fact, after 1948, two populations were not mobilized: ultra-Orthodox Jews and Arabs. Ultra-Orthodox Jews were not mobilized because of agreements reached between the rabbinical leaders of the community who opposed their young people being drafted because they would be exposed to modern, non-religious society and would not pursue lives of Torah study. In practice, young men enrolled in Torah study were not drafted. This situation was formalized in the Tal Law in 2002. Arabs were not drafted because they were seen as being identified with "the enemy" and unlikely to be loyal.

Recent talk of drafting ultra-Orthodox and Arabs has been the result of the ruling in 2012 that determined that the Tal Law was not in accord with the Basic Laws and the ensuing popular movement among Israeli citizens that all should serve in the army.

In 1956, the Israeli authorities reached an agreement with the Druze religious leadership. It stated that young non-religious Druze, also known as the *juhhal* who are ignorant of religious teaching, would be drafted. It also stated that the religious youth known as the *uqqal* who are initiated into religious teaching, would be exempt under a similar understanding of the ultra-Orthodox community. In return, the Israeli authorities recognized the Druze religious leadership as totally

---

[3] This includes Jerusalem Arab residents. The past months have seen a rise in the attempts to draft some Jerusalem Christians into the military. Here we deal only with Arab citizens of Israel.

independent from Muslim leadership and instituted a separate religious court system. Circassian Muslims were drafted in 1958. Various Bedouin tribes from Galilee and from Naqab (Negev) also agreed to the mobilization of their young men, although no general conscription of the Bedouin exists.

As early as the 1950s, some Israeli officials promoted the mobilization of all Arabs. Others focused on the Christian Arabs. Draft orders were in fact served to the young Christians in Jish, a village with a large Maronite population. The draft orders were not followed up, probably because the Arab Christians were still seen as a security threat due to their being part of the general Arab population and enjoying a high level of education.

Why Does Israel Seek to Mobilize the Christians Today?
Israel does not need more soldiers in an age of technological warfare. However, the military is seen as an institution that promotes social cohesion – a very important melting pot in the Israeli reality of diversity. The army is seen as a principal place of forming "national Israeli-Zionist" consciousness and participating in the nation building project as conceived by the authorities. An example of this is the promoting of Israel as a Jewish national state. Army service is seen as a tool to promote the Israelization of the Arab minority. Identification with Israel, rather than with Palestinian Arab society, is clearly an important goal.

The mobilization of minorities is undoubtedly also motivated by the will "to divide and rule" the Arab minority. By drafting some segments of the population, the authorities succeed in dividing the society. This was clearly the case with the mobilization of Druze, Bedouin and Circassian minorities, who were defined by government offices as "non-Arab." Talk about drafting the Christian Arabs rather than the Arabs in general that include Muslims and Christians, is clearly an attempt to drive a wedge between Christian and Muslim Arabs in Israel.

Why Do Some Christians Serve in the Israeli Army?

Non-Arab Christians are regularly drafted into the military. Since 1996, with the increase of non-Arab Russian speaking Christians being drafted, Christian soldiers were even allowed to swear the oath of loyalty on a copy of the New Testament. Christian soldiers can ask for leave on Christian holidays. It is also true that extensive pressure is exerted on non-Jewish soldiers, particularly those integrated into the Hebrew speaking, Jewish population by the rabbinate within the military to convert to Judaism. Extensive conversion courses also are offered.

Some Christian Arabs do volunteer for army service along with some Muslim Arabs. Their motivations are usually either economic because the army provides well paid employment to professional soldiers, or professional because the belief that educational, occupational and other social opportunities, otherwise off limits to Arabs, will open up after army service. There is also a belief among some who serve in the army that if Arabs fulfill this duty, they will receive equal rights to those of the Jewish population. This will be strengthened if the parliament passes proposed legislation now being debated. This legislation offers certain privileges to those who serve in the army, specifically employment in the bureaucracy of the state.

It is important to note that the drive towards volunteering for army service among Christian Arabs is particularly strong after manifestations of confessional (Christian-Druze or Christian-Muslim) tension. This can be seen in the relatively higher number of Christians being drafted in certain areas, such as Kafr Yassif, which borders on the Druze village of Julis, where the residents are Druze and serve in the military, or in Maghar where tensions within the village between Druze and Christians have erupted in violence in recent years.

What Should be the Position of the Church?

Clearly the Church teaches that Christians should be good citizens and participate actively in society to promote the common good. The Church is committed to raise consciousness about issues of justice, reconciliation, love of enemies and non-violence, as well as the ethical problems of war.

In her promotion of awareness of justice issues, the Church should point out that the Israeli army is used as an instrument promoting the interests of only one part of the population, the Jews, to the detriment of the Palestinians. The army is used as a means of imposing and maintaining the occupation of Palestinian lands. Thus, it prevents the Palestinians from achieving dignity and independence. The army is primarily an army of aggression rather than an army of defense. This is clear in its patrolling of the Palestinian areas and its defense of the settlers.[4]

Furthermore, in promoting an awareness of the rights to equality, the Church can point out that Israel discriminates against her Arab citizens. The case of the Druze and Bedouin is a particularly powerful testimony to the fact that army service does not bring equality. The Druze and many Bedouin have been serving for decades in the Israeli army and yet their villages are still grossly underdeveloped when compared with neighboring Jewish areas.[5] In fact, as Druze became better educated, their resistance to the draft has grown. Since 1972, the Druze Initiative Committee has actively promoted refusal to serve in the army and is assisting Druze youngsters who are imprisoned for this refusal.

---

[4] The term settlers here is used to refer to those who participate in the illegal colonization of territories beyond the internationally recognized borders of Israel, in the West Bank, including East Jerusalem, and the Golan Heights.

[5] In fact, despite military service, Bedouin villages are being destroyed, and others struggle for recognition in order to receive the most basic services in the state.

The Church promotes good neighborly relations within the Arab minority, which includes Christians, Muslims, Druze and all others. The use of army service to divide the Arab population against itself is detrimental to the interests of the Arabs as a community. The promotion of army service among the less educated and more impoverished must be countered with the promotion of better education, improved social conditions, more cohesion within the Arab minority in Israel and a concerted struggle for equality in the State of Israel.

Furthermore, the Church is also aware that many Arab youth in Israel are losing their national, cultural and religious identity. Many no longer identify themselves as Arabs. In some places, such as the mixed cities of Jaffa, Ramleh, Haifa, Lydda, etc., many young Christian Arabs try their best to assimilate into the Jewish majority and identify with it. The Church sees her task as one of educating our young people to accept themselves as they are, giving them a balanced human, national and Christian education. This includes an awareness of their history, their rootedness in the land, and a sense of identity that integrates the different elements of the Palestinian Arab, Christian and citizen of Israel, rather than repressing any one of these elements. The bishops and priests must help the faithful in the midst of this "crisis of identity."

What about Proposals Regarding Civil Rather than Military Service?

Faced with the understandable reticence of some Arabs to take up arms against their brothers and sisters, the Israeli authorities have been proposing some kind of civil service for Arab residents. What needs to be made clear is:

- Civil service in the format proposed is equivalent to military service, and therefore, equally problematic along the lines underlined above.
- The military authorities are those initiating the option to do civil service with the same goals of legitimizing the status quo and promoting a "national"

consciousness that is opposed to the aspirations of the Palestinian Arab people.

- Despite the benign appearance of the forms of civil service proposed, the underlying principle behind this form of civil service is the defense of the "Jewish" character of the state to the detriment of those citizens and residents who are Palestinian. The forms of civil service proposed in this framework only maintain the existing occupation of Palestinian land and discrimination against Palestinian Arabs in Israel.

The members of the Commission of Justice and Peace of the Assembly of Catholic Ordinaries in the Holy Land ask that the Catholic Ordinaries address the many issues that face the faithful in their daily lives, including the complex socio-political issues in the State of Israel.

6. An Attempt to Divide Palestinian Christians
September 16, 2014

The Israeli Ministry of the Interior announced that Christian Palestinian Arab citizens in Israel can now change their registration in the Ministry from Arabs to "Arameans." What does this mean? Arameans were an ancient people that lived in the Middle East. Their language, Aramaic, was the lingua franca of the Assyrian, Babylonian and Persian Empires. It was adopted by the Jews in the Babylonian Exile and has remained important for them even today because a large part of the rabbinic tradition was written in Aramaic. Some streams of Christianity adopted a form of Aramaic, known as Syriac, and it remains a liturgical language for some Eastern Churches still.

Arabs who live today in Greater Syria have spoken different languages over the centuries: Aramaic, Greek and Arabic. Today, the unique language in daily use throughout the area is Arabic, except for tiny pockets where some form of colloquial Aramaic is preserved. Today, we, in Israel are Christian Palestinians Arabs.

Some in the Israeli administration seem to think that separating Christian Palestinians from other Palestinians is a way to protect Christians. We say to these people, if you are sincere, first, give us back our homes, our properties, our villages and towns – all that you have confiscated. Second, the best way to protect us is to keep us in our people. Third, the best protection for us, for you and for all, is to seriously engage in walking the path of peace.

To those who seek to change our identity, we say, you can gain our support as allies uniquely in the way of peace. We are allies for peace without you needing to take invasive measures to dilute our identity. In fact, all Palestinians can be allies for peace, but a peace based on respect for human dignity. For many today, the Israeli administration is the one who refuses peace.

If you chose to remain on the path of war, do not push us to follow you. The way of war is not our way. It is a way that benefits nobody, neither you nor us, nor anybody in the region. We cannot be condemned, neither us nor you, nor any human being, to live in a permanent state of war. If your choice is war in order to remain the stronger party, leave us with our choice of peace. We will act for peace, for us and for you, for all our people, and for all the region.

To the few Christian Palestinian Arabs in Israel, who support this idea of changing their identity or serving in the Israeli army, we say, come back to your senses. Do not harm your people, because of idle promises and personal egoistic gain. By adopting such a position, you do not benefit yourselves, nor do you benefit Israel. Israel is in need of Christians who have heard Jesus' teaching of "Blessed the peace makers." Israel does not need Christians who have deformed their identity, who position themselves as enemy of their own people and who become soldiers for war. This does not produce peace, neither for you, nor for any other Israeli. Serve yourselves, serve your people and serve Israel in remaining faithful to the truth – faithful to your identity as Christians, as Palestinians and as peacemakers. Promote peace among yourselves, among Palestinians and Israelis.

The vocation of the Christian is not to suddenly become an Aramean, nor to go to war. Rather, the vocation of the Christian is to point the way to peace and to walk in its path. This peace must be built on the dignity of each human being, Palestinian and Jewish. Blessed are the peacemakers for they truly serve God and humanity – all humanity, Palestinians and Israelis and the whole region.

7. Elections in Israel: Voters, Be Responsible and Vote

February 11, 2015

On March 17, 2015 national elections will be held in Israel.

We say to the voters and to the elected that we are deeply concerned about justice, peace and equality in this country. We care about the human being, whoever he or she is. We promote the mutual acceptance of one and all, facilitating life in justice, peace, tranquility, prosperity and solidarity.

In order to progress towards these aims, we call upon the voters to go out and vote in the upcoming elections. We call upon those who might tend to abstain and thus remain silent to exercise their vote. Your vote, your single vote, might make a difference for our present and future in this country and in the lives of many. Take up your responsibility and vote according to your conscience. Vote, and thus speak out. Your voice is important.

We hope that those who will be elected will hear the voices of all who suffer in this permanent conflict. Your duty is to help the country emerge from the enduring situation of conflict. We are not condemned to live forever in fear of the other and in continuous suffering. Help make this holy land a better place. The great and the powerful are those who can bring back tranquility to this country. All of us together can build a better world for all.

8. Christmas Message, Christmas, 2015

This year, Christmas approaches and darkness surrounds us. Hatred, violence and death engulf our land and our region. Forces of darkness named occupation, discrimination, religious fanaticism and intolerance continue to dominate our world and our daily lives. Walls are built. Homes are destroyed. Families are separated. Land is confiscated and siege is imposed. Anger grows and fear reigns. **Too many Palestinians** have lost hope, and in their despair, go out to wound or to kill, and ultimately to be killed. Too many Israelis believe that in killing they will have security. This is our reality in this land called to be holy. What can we say at Christmas time? How can we continue to hope?

Into such a world, 2,000 years ago, a small child was born. Indeed, His world and ours are remarkably similar. As he walked in it, we walk in it. As we kneel before Him and offer Him homage, we want to reaffirm that we are His disciples. He is vulnerable. He is weak. He is needy. And yet, He shows us the way. He, too, will be swallowed up by the darkness, but God will not allow the darkness to have the last word. This is our faith. This Christmas, we affirm that light will conquer darkness, that truth will vanquish deceit and that justice and peace will come. He will not bring peace by waving a magic wand, but He will empower us to remain steadfast and work for justice and peace.

After the Resurrection, the disciples continued to live in a hostile world. Their faith consoled them, but they continued to cry out: "how long will it be?" (Revelation 6:10) Together with them, today we take up their cry. For decades, our land has been awash in blood, and the latest round of violence is ferocious and pitiless. Yet, in the midst of all this, and without ignoring what surrounds us, we want to affirm that we will continue! We will not give up! Yes, all solutions seem to have failed. All ideologies seem to be bankrupt. All those who have worked to bring justice and peace, whether the United Nations, the Arab states, the United States, the European Union, have floundered as the Israeli government resolutely affirms its conviction that military might will eventually conquer. But, **we know, it** will never bring the solution.

We will continue to live and fight injustice, fear and violence! We will continue to speak out and look tirelessly for reasons to hope! We will continue to resist the darkness! Some might say this hoping against hope is futile and an illusion! We respond that God is almighty and merciful and loves his **children**. The hour of mercy and justice among people will come when we do not expect it. Moreover, we remember the word of the Psalmist, *"For a thousand years in God's sight are like yesterday when it is past, or like a watch in the night."* (Psalm 90:4) As we prepare to welcome the newborn Child, we recommit to remain faithful to His teaching until He comes again, appearing in His goodness and **with the justice and peace** for which we wait. Furthermore, we recommit to work with others, bringing new energy and creativity in order to promote life in this situation of death. We do this as individual disciples of Christ within our societies as we affirm that every human being is stronger **than** the power of death that surrounds us. We also recommit in the name of our churches, our schools, our universities, our hospitals, our homes for the elderly, the handicapped and the marginal, and our associations for life, human rights, conflict resolution and dialogue. These institutions are oases of life, open to everybody. They already show a way in the darkness!

At this time of Christmas, we say that we will continue to live right at the heart of the darkness while resisting this darkness with courage and conviction. We will continue to raise our children to love and promote life. We will continue to believe that it need not be this way. We will continue to be witnesses to the Child who is born as Prince of Peace. In this spirit, we wish one and all a Christmas of hope and light!

9. A New Vision
February 3, 2016

The Commission for Justice and Peace met in its ordinary meeting on February 3, 2016, in Jerusalem, and reflected on the present political situation. It reflected on the human and ethical aspects and addressed the following message.

The situation is stagnant and lifeless, with no light of hope: not for the Israelis, who need security and tranquility; neither for the Palestinians, who wait for the end of the Occupation and an independent state.

The present situation for the Palestinians is inhuman. It is one of settlers who occupy, day after day, Palestinian land. It is the siege of Gaza for years already. One and a half million are under a siege of poverty, misery and humiliation. It is also a siege for the rest of Palestine with diverse political, economic and social hardships. It is the demolishing of homes. It includes military checkpoints and the arbitrary behavior of Israeli soldiers humiliating the Palestinian. These checkpoints are a place of humiliation. They are constructed uniquely on the logic of war and are a place that magnifies hatred and death daily. It is the siege of Jerusalem, the Judaization of the city and the sending away of its Palestinian inhabitants. It is the all-inclusive accusation of terrorism against all Palestinians and the collective punishment that results from it. Today, the situation has become a new Intifada in which Palestinians are without hope and plunge to their death out of despair caused by a life full of frustration, humiliation and insecurity. Is Israeli society satisfied with this situation? Is it satisfied with this life in the shadow of continuing hostility with the Palestinian people?

We see that the situation is inhuman and cannot be what the Israelis would choose. It is neither the choice of the Palestinians. Change must take place. We say to the leaders that they act for the sake of the human being – the Israeli and the Palestinian. Do not leave the situation as it is because it is a situation that leads to death. Do not say, Palestinians are terrorists. Palestinians are people who seek to live a normal life. Instead they find themselves oppressed, frustrated and deprived of the freedom God has given them. You, Israelis you want to live in security and tranquility. The Palestinians also want to live the same kind of life. What is the obstacle preventing this? Political leaders? Or their incapacity to find a practical solution that corresponds to the desire of the Israelis and the Palestinians? Both peoples can live together in peace and tranquility.

We say to the Israelis leaders to enlarge your vision and your hearts. Change the situation. Shake it out of its immobility. There is enough space in the land for us all. Let all have the same dignity and equality. No occupation and no discrimination. Two peoples living together and loving each other according to the way they choose. They are able to love each other and to make peace together.

To the Palestinian leaders, we say to let the people of Israel and the world hear one unique voice, a voice of peace and justice for two peoples. Redeem the land again and begin a new history. Redeem Jerusalem again, and begin a new history that conforms with its holiness and universality. Stop every self-interested vision and all corruption.

To fulfill this, we need re-education of our future generations. It is necessary for the Israeli generations who have grown up with the unique vision that Palestinians are all terrorists and for the Palestinian generations who have grown up seeing in the Israeli only an enemy. Let all of us begin a new history. Our land is holy and the place of our daily living together. Let the two peoples live together in peace.

10. Beyond Occupation and Confrontation: Towards a Common Understanding
March 21, 2016

In a report published on March 8, 2016, by the renown Pew Research Center, entitled "Israel's Religiously Divided Society," it was revealed that almost half of the Jewish Israeli population support the idea of expelling or transferring the Arabs from Israel. In reaction, Israel State President Reuven Rivlin urged that the survey be "placed before the decision makers in Israel," and said it "must serve as a wake-up call for Israeli society, to bring about some soul-searching and moral reflection." (Times of Israel, 8.3.2016) The study showed that Israeli society is deeply divided, socially, politically and religiously. It showed that Israel today is less democratic, less egalitarian and less free than it has ever been.

The report shows that one of the main issues facing Israeli society is the Israeli occupation of Palestine. The report said the future of the process must ultimately bring justice and peace for Israelis and Palestinians alike. Meanwhile, Palestinian resistance continues, dubbed "the stabbing Intifada." Five months have passed in which over thirty Israelis, four foreign nationals and over one hundred and eighty Palestinians have been killed. Two thirds of the Palestinians were shot while allegedly attacking Israelis. The rest were killed in clashes that have erupted between youth and the Israeli military.

We continue to cry out like the prophets did "Until when oh Lord?" (cf. Habbakuk 1:2, Zechariah 1:12, Revelation 6:10) We repeat again that we, as disciples of Christ, condemn violence on all sides. Violence is violence. Violence only begets more violence. We, as created in the image and likeness of our Father, need to learn another way to solve the conflict.

Why has this conflict gone on for so long? Is it really so complicated? Jews in Palestine and throughout the world succeeded in establishing a state in 1948 on 78% of the territory of Palestine. The Palestinians did not succeed in establishing a state. In 1967, Israel occupied the remaining 22% of Palestine. These lands are still occupied or surrounded and under siege. A Palestinian state only exists as a dream. A large number of Israelis declare that they do not want to be occupiers, and Palestinians demand an end to the occupation.

Ending the occupation depends largely on the occupier. Why is Israel not working to end the occupation? It is only ending the occupation that will ultimately put an end to violence – the violence of the occupier and the occupied alike.

The occupier speaks about the incitement fueled by the occupied. Can this really be a justification to maintain the occupation? What is defined as incitement includes parents telling their children the history of their people, the genesis and ongoing saga of the Palestinian exile. Palestinians indeed tell their children that Israel is the enemy and Israelis tell their children exactly the same thing. Sadly, we are at war. Anyway, it is not incitement that is the ultimate cause of the problem.

The root cause of the problem is occupation, which is deprivation of freedom and human dignity. The only way to end supposed incitement and teaching new generations about the "enemy" is to end occupation. Only the occupier can do that!

There are those who talk peace and seek dialogue. There are those on both sides, who despite everything, refuse to stop dreaming. We welcome those and embrace them. However, on the ground, decisions are made that strengthen separation, discrimination, exclusion and exile. Despite the hopeful words of some, the laws, the military ordinances, the demagoguery of politicians, the assassinations, the arrests, the land confiscations, the family separation and the daily frustrations have led to hopelessness. These have also led to the eruption of violence, in particular among young people who are convinced that they have nothing to lose because they see no future.

We are called to speak out again and again. We have no political or military force, but we do have voices to be used to name things by their names and to call for responsibility. We have the responsibility to remind one and all that we are all human beings. We mourn every death by violence from both sides. We need to constantly renew the dream that there can be justice and peace for all. We believe in a kingdom of God that is already among us and not yet manifest. In this kingdom there are no enemies, but only brothers of one loving Father. In this kingdom, there are no borders, no walls, no fences. There is only one holy land in which people talk peace with one another. We refuse to be silent, and we refuse to stop hoping.

11. Prisoners' Hunger Strike
April 29, 2017

"He has sent me to proclaim liberty to the captives." (Lk 4: 18)
"I was in prison and you came to see me." (Mt 25: 36)

More than 1,500 out of 6,500 Palestinian political prisoners have begun an open hunger strike, initiated on April 17,2017. The aim of this desperate act is to shed light, both locally and internationally, on the inhuman conditions in which they are detained by the Israeli Authorities. They plead for the respect of their human rights and dignity as recognized by international law and the Geneva Convention and the end of administrative detention.

The Justice and Peace Commission of the Assembly of the Catholic Ordinaries of the Holy Land affirms the necessity of the application of international law with regard to political prisoners. It condemns the use of detention without trial and all forms of collective punishment, as well as the use of duress and torture for whatever reason. Furthermore, we can never forget that every prisoner is a human being, and his God given dignity must be respected.

We urge the Israeli Authorities to hear the cry of the prisoners, to respect their human dignity and to open a new door towards the making of peace. The liberation of prisoners will be a sign of a new vision. It will also be the beginning of a new history for both Israeli and Palestinian peoples.

As Christians, we are sent to work for the liberation of every human being and for the establishment of a human society in which there is equality for all Israelis and Palestinians.

12. The Question of Normalization
May 14, 2017

What is normalization in the Israel-Palestine context? At its most basic level, "normalization" is the establishment of relations with the State of Israel, its organisms and citizens "as if" the current situation is a normal state of affairs, thus ignoring ongoing war, occupation and discrimination, or consciously obscuring or marginalizing them.

The subject of "normalization" constitutes an important part of the political debate in the Arab world today, and most especially in Palestine, concerning attitudes to adopt towards the State of Israel. Opposition to normalization and accusations of normalization are heard regularly with regard to governments, non-governmental organizations and individuals.

In fact, the political situation in Israel-Palestine is far from normal, due to the ongoing conflict between two peoples, Palestinians and Israelis. This conflict has a profound impact on daily life in the two different entities, the State of Palestine and the State of Israel defined by the pre-1967 borders.

In the State of Israel, all citizens, Jews and Arabs, have equal rights in principle. In reality, Arab citizens are discriminated against in various fields and in various ways. This includes in access to development, education, jobs and public funding for Arab municipalities, etc. Some of these forms of discrimination are embedded in legislation, but others are indirect and hidden.

In the State of Palestine, in spite of the existence of the Palestinian Authority, Palestinians continue to live under military occupation, which determines their daily life. It determines settlement and road building, legalization of Israeli construction on private Palestinian land, military incursions, assassinations, arbitrary arrests, administrative detention and collective punishment, confiscation of land and destruction of houses. Checkpoints as part of the occupation limit the freedom of movement and create numerous obstacles for economic development. It even prevents family reunification, a violation of the natural right of members of the same nuclear family to cohabitate together.

In both societies, Israeli and Palestinian, the life of the Palestinians is far from normal, and acting "as if" things were normal ignores the violation of fundamental human rights. At the same time, in both situations, daily life requires certain relations with the Israeli Authorities. However, all persons and institutions involved in maintaining these relations should be aware that something "abnormal" needs to be set right, rather than allowing the "abnormal" to become the order of the day.

In Israel, Arabs who hold Israeli citizenship, interact with the civil authorities and are represented in the Knesset. There are over 300,000 Christians who live in Israel. These include Arab citizens of Israel, Hebrew-speaking Christian citizens of Israel and long-term resident labor migrants and asylum seekers. Citizens and long-term residents are law abiding, yet they have the right and the moral obligation to use all available legal and non-violent means to promote full rights and complete equality for all citizens. Ignoring or marginalizing this duty is "normalization," and collaborating with structures of discrimination, and it leads to, the permanence of injustice and the lack of peace. Within this context, the Church is obligated to ensure the smooth running of parishes, schools and many other institutions, obligating interactions with all those that administer the territories within which the Church is active. This, however, must never obscure the Church's commitment to justice and her denunciation of all injustice.

In Palestine, the Palestinian Authority is compelled to coordinate with the Israeli Authorities in order to be able to function. Yet, Palestinian citizens have very limited control over their own lives and need Israeli permits and approval for many aspects of daily existence. This includes visiting the Holy Places in occupied Jerusalem, building homes and businesses in Israeli-controlled areas of Palestine and having access to Palestinian institutions, such as parishes, schools, hospitals in occupied Jerusalem. The Church as well, for the requirements of her daily life, cannot live and work without applying to the Israeli Authorities for permits and visas. The Church has the moral obligation to constantly discern between what is unavoidable in maintaining relations with the occupying power to ensure these daily necessities and what must be avoided, such as engaging in relations and activities that promote a consciousness that "the situation is normal."

The Church, given the nature of her mission, has her own values and criteria to define her position in a situation of conflict like the one in Israel-Palestine. No single brand of political discourse, no particular party position, nor any particular ideological option binds the Church. At the same time, the Church cannot ignore fundamental injustice or acts that endanger peace and the welfare of the human person. By her very nature, the Church opposes occupation and discrimination. The Church is committed to promote justice and peace, as well as the unique dignity and equality of every human person. The Church can never ignore injustice "as if" all is well. The Church is obligated to speak out, resist evil and work tirelessly for change. Like the prophets of old, the Church, a prophetic body, points out injustice and denounces it.

There is, therefore, an important intersection between political discourse that opposes normalization and the Church's position with regard to situations of injustice. The Church works with all who share the values she proclaims; whatever human group they might belong to, whether Palestinian or Israeli. The Church seeks and encourages dialogue with all people, including Israelis, as well as individuals and organizations who recognize the need to end the occupation and eliminate discrimination. The Church is committed to identifying these individuals and organizations who do not perpetuate the situation by presuming that dialogue or cooperation can ignore the struggle to achieve justice, thus hiding the unjust realities that define the daily lives of those living under occupation or those facing the restraints of discrimination. The Church is committed to identifying partners and developing constructive strategies in collaboration with them to repair our broken world. Furthermore, the Local Church in Israel-Palestine has the responsibility of reminding the Universal Church that Israel-Palestine is an open, festering wound, and that the situation cannot be considered normal.

In the present, confused and hopeless political situation, Christian communities, Church leaders and individual believers are in need of ongoing discernment. They are invited to consult and work together to find the best ways to testify to a just and equal society for all, while cultivating respectful relations with all their fellow citizens, with whom they are called to live together and working together for a lasting and just peace.

13. Defining Terminology
February 12, 2018

The beginning of wisdom is the definition of terms.
Socrates

Words have enormous power. This is especially true in situations of conflict. We believe that it is important to define a few terms that are too often confused in popular discourse in Palestine and throughout the Middle East today.

Christian, Evangelical, Crusader, Messianic

Christians are an integral part of Palestinian society, and in particular Arab society in general. Confusion of language can harm the fabric of our society where the unity of citizens must also be based upon the respect of difference.

Christian: A Christian is a believer in Jesus of Nazareth as Christ. He or she is a member of the community of believers, called the Church. The Church was born in Jerusalem in the first century. As the Church spread throughout the area of the Middle East, the name *"Christian"* was first given to this group of believers in Antioch. (cf. Acts of the Apostles 11:26) From Jerusalem and Antioch, the Church continued to spread to the furthest extents of the earth, bringing into its fold people from every nation, race and language. There is a rich diversity of Christians that include Byzantine, Latin, Armenian Coptic, Syriac, Ethiopic as well as Christian communities born in recent centuries in Europe. Each group lives its tradition and cultural heritage within an array of expressions.

Evangelical: The word means *"belonging to the Gospel."* However, in the modern period, this word often refers to a current within Christianity that preaches a "return" to the Gospel, often opposing the traditional Church and sometimes insisting on a fundamentalist reading of the Bible. Among these

Evangelicals, there are those who developed a Zionist political ideology based upon a fundamentalist reading of the Bible. They see in the State of Israel, the supposed fulfillment of biblical prophecies and a sign of the end of times, when Christ will return and put an end to the world as we know it.

Crusader: The term refers to a series of invasions of the Middle East, which began in 1095 and ended in 1291. These wars originated in Europe when Christians were roused to try and liberate the Tomb of Christ from Muslim rule. The Crusades were inspired by a dangerous mixture of faith, politics, war and colonization. In 2000, Pope John Paul II, in a liturgy asking forgiveness for the sins of Christians, prayed: *"Lord of the world, Father of all, through your Son, you asked us to love our enemies, to do good to those who hate us and to pray for those who persecute us. Yet Christians have often denied the Gospel; yielding to a mentality of power, they have violated the rights of ethnic groups and peoples, and shown contempt for their cultures and religious traditions: be patient and merciful towards us, and grant us your forgiveness!"* Today, the word "Crusader" is often used, in particular in some Muslim circles, to denounce aggressive political intervention by the West in the affairs of the Middle East.

Messianic: In its original sense, Messianic means to believe that the Messiah is about to come or has already come. In modern political terms, this word has been used to describe radical political movements that justify or even promote violence in the name of a religious-political ideology. Among those who support Zionism, the term can refer to both Jews and Christians who believe that the State of Israel is a sign that the Messiah is coming for Jews or coming again for Christians. They believe that the State of Israel should be fully supported in the battle against its supposed enemies.

Jew, Israeli, Zionist and Messianic Jew

The word "Jew" has become a loaded term because of the ongoing Israel-Palestine conflict. It is important not to lose sight of what this word and other related words mean.

Jew: A Jew is someone who practices the Jewish religion and/or sees himself or herself as belonging to the Jewish people. There is a great debate among Jews about what constitutes their identity. The religion and culture of the Jews originated in this area, and Jews have always been a part of the peoples of Palestine and the Middle East. However, Jews migrated from Palestine and settled all over the world, spreading their religion. Before 1850, there was a small community of Jews in Palestine, part and parcel of the Palestinian population made up of Muslims, Christians and Jews. The vast majority of the Jews, who live in Israel-Palestine today, have their family origins in Europe, North Africa and North America.

Israeli: An Israeli is a citizen of the State of Israel. Today, Israeli citizens include a majority of Jews at about 76%, and a large group of Palestinian Arabs, who are Muslim, Christian and Druze. There is also a small number of other groups considered to be Israelis.

Zionist: A Zionist is the proponent of a political ideology that propagates the idea that the Jews have the right to "*a homeland*" in historical Palestine. Although Zionism has roots in Christian Biblical fundamentalism in the 17th century, it emerged as an organized Jewish political institution at the end of the 19th century. It acted as a form of European colonialism with European Jews arriving in Palestine and building settlements until the aftermath of the Second World War. It was then, in the light of the Holocaust, that the majority of Jews and the international community began to support the aims of Zionism. The success of Zionism in the establishment of the State of Israel led to the exile of the majority of Palestinians from their homeland. Those that remain have been subject to discrimination and occupation.

Messianic Jew: A Messianic Jew is a Jew who believes that Jesus of Nazareth is the Christ, the Messiah, and that the Gospel is the fulfillment of the Scriptures of Israel. Although Messianic Jews tend not to belong to any Christian Church, many of them are affiliated with or supported by Evangelical Christians.

14. On the Demolition of Khan al-Ahmar
October 6, 2018

Since the 1980s, Israel has been actively attempting to transfer the Jahalin Bedouin from their homes in East Jerusalem to areas in the vicinity of Jericho. The reason for this transfer is to allow for the expansion of Jewish settlements established after 1967 around Jerusalem. This planned ring of settlements around Jerusalem will effectively sever Arab East Jerusalem from the West Bank, preventing the establishment of a Palestinian state with its capital in East Jerusalem. The demolition of Khan al-Ahmar has been repeatedly delayed, in part because of international concern and pressure. However, the Israeli authorities have proclaimed their determination to carry out the planned action, by force if necessary.

After a long period of legal struggle, the Israeli Supreme Court ruled that the Israeli Authorities are entitled to demolish the Bedouin village at Khan al-Ahmar and areas nearby, as well as the transfer of its residents to an area near Jericho. This is a disaster for the residents of this village. It is also a real threat for many other locations the Israeli authorities seek to demolish for similar reasons, including the Bedouin living at Jabal al-Baba, Wadi al-Hindi, Al-Muntar, Abu Nuwar, Wadi al-Awaj, etc. In fact, the Bedouin in the Jerusalem area are victims of a policy that is also being implemented in the Naqab (Negev), in the south of Israel and in places like Umm al-Hiran and elsewhere. This policy promotes the displacement of Bedouin and the construction of Jewish settlements.

The Justice and Peace Commission of the Assembly of Catholic Ordinaries of the Holy Land strongly condemn this action, which totally ignores the rights of thousands of Bedouin to live in peace, justice and dignity. Many of these people were already displaced after the 1948 war and are now, once again, being violently uprooted to make way for more illegal Israeli settlements.

The Commission points out that Israel is a signatory on the Geneva Convention, in which paragraph 4-f prohibits the transfer of civil population in military occupied territory. This would not only imply that the Bedouin cannot be removed from their lands, but also that the plan to bring Israeli settlers to populate this land is illegal. It is regrettable that the Israeli Supreme Court has found it necessary to declare legal an action that is blatantly illegal. The Bedouin were blocked from obtaining the necessary permits to stay on and develop their lands, whereas Jewish Israeli settlers are encouraged to consider such lands their own and to develop them.

The Commission calls on Israelis, who are concerned about justice and peace, as well as the international community, to protest this violation of international law and demand protection for the Bedouin and their rights. The Justice and Peace Commission affirms the right of every human person to his land and place of residence. This is a natural and human right no state should violate. The Holy Land cries out for justice and humanity in the face of attempts to displace populations and replace them with others. This activity of displacement and replacement is an ongoing process throughout occupied Palestine and within parts of the State of Israel, too. Our land is called to be a holy land, a land of justice and peace. We are called to join hands and work together for more humanity, more democracy, more equality and more respect for every human being.

15. On the Nation State Law Passed by the Israeli Knesset

October 31, 2018

In the spirit of dialogue, the Assembly of the Catholic Ordinaries of the Holy Land wishes to address the issue of the Nation State Law passed by the Israeli Knesset on July 19, 2018.

According to this law, the State of Israel has legislated that the people, whose "welfare and safety" it is most concerned to promote and protect, are limited to the Jewish citizens of the State of Israel. We must draw the attention of the authorities to a simple fact. That is our faithful, the Christians, and our fellow citizens, Muslim, Druze and Baha'i, all of us who are Arabs, are no less citizens of this country than our Jewish brothers and sisters.

Since the promulgation of the Declaration of Independence in May 1948, the Arab citizens of the State of Israel have noted the tension that exists in the wording of the declaration about the State being both "Jewish" and "democratic." Whereas the ever-changing equilibrium between these two terms has been worked out predominantly by the Jewish majority, the Arab minority has been struggling against all manifestations of discrimination whenever the "Jewish" element outbalanced the "democratic" one. This has meant an ongoing struggle and careful vigilance to protect the rights of all citizens, as well as to guarantee as much as possible the values of equality, justice and democracy. The 1992 Israeli Knesset promulgation of the Basic Law: Human Dignity and Liberty was a milestone in the struggle to protect and promote these values.

However, the 2018 Israeli Knesset promulgation of the Basic Law: Israel as the Nation State of the Jewish People is a blow to these values. Although the law changes very little in practice, it does provide a constitutional and legal basis for discrimination among Israel's citizens. It clearly lays out the principles according to which Jewish citizens are to be privileged over and above other citizens. By promulgating "the development of Jewish settlement as a national value and will act to encourage and promote its establishment and consolidation," the law promotes an inherent discriminatory vision. In fact, other than seriously downgrading the standing of the Arab language in relationship to the Hebrew language, the law totally ignores the fact that there is another people, the Palestinian Arabs, and other major religious communities, Christians and Muslims, as well as Druze and Baha'i, that are profoundly rooted in this land.

Christians, Muslims, Druze, Baha'i and Jews demand to be treated as equal citizens. This equality must include the respectful recognition of our civic (Israeli), ethnic (Palestinian Arab) and religious (Christian) identities, as both individuals and as communities. As Israelis and as Palestinian Arabs, we seek to be part of a state that promotes justice and peace, security and prosperity for all its citizens. As Christians, we take pride that the universal Church was founded in Jerusalem, and in that her first faithful were children of this land and its people. We recognize that Jerusalem and the whole of this holy land is a heritage we share with Jews, Muslims, Druze and Baha'i. It is a heritage we are called upon to protect from division and internecine strife.

This Basic Law contradicts the identifiable humanist and democratic strands in Israeli legislation, as well as international laws and conventions to which Israel is signatory, having as their aim the promotion of human rights, the respect of diversity and the strengthening of justice, equality and peace. We, as the religious leaders of the Catholic Churches, call on the authorities to rescind this Basic Law and assure one and all that the State of Israel seeks to promote and protect the welfare and the safety of all its citizens.

16. Righteousness and Peace Will Kiss Each Other

(May 20, 2019)

Let me hear what God the Lord will speak, for he will speak peace to his people, to his faithful, to those who turn to him in their hearts. Surely his salvation is at hand for those who fear him, that his glory may dwell in our land. Steadfast love and faithfulness will meet; righteousness and peace will kiss each other. Faithfulness will spring up from the ground, and righteousness will look down from the sky. (Psalm 85:8-11)

The recent developments in the Palestine-Israel context, which includes the ongoing loss of lives, the continuing evaporation of hope for a durable solution and the failure of the international community to insist on the application of international law to save the peoples of this land from more struggle and despair, have reached a point where we witness more extremism and discrimination. Even those, who once presented themselves as guardians of democracy and promoters of peace, have become powerbrokers and partisan participants in the conflict.

This has led many to question whether international diplomacy and the peace process were ever actually based on justice and good will. Many in Palestine and in Israel feel that since the launch of the peace process, their lives have become more and more unbearable. Many have left. Many more consider leaving, and some are resorting to violence. Some die quietly and others are losing faith and hope.

Reflecting on the past few decades during which we were promised peace and reconciliation but received more hatred and oppression, corruption and demagoguery, it is time for the Churches and spiritual leaders to point to another way. We need to insist that all, Israelis and Palestinians, are brothers and sisters in humanity. The Churches insist that we can love one another and live together in this same land in mutual respect and equality, equal in rights and duties. This is not simply a dream but the powerful basis of a vision that inspired our ancestors, the prophets.

Only a peace based on dignity, mutual respect and equality as human beings will save us. Only this will allow us to survive, and even thrive, in this land made holy by the witness of our ancestors, patriarchs and prophets, and which we continue to make holy by our striving for justice, our thirst for peace and the mutual love we have for one another. We are in need of a new orientation, a new education and a new vision for this land and the two peoples who live here.

We, the heads of the Catholic Churches in the Holy Land, stand with all those living in the land, first and foremost, as human beings. We seek to show a way out of a permanent situation of war, hatred and death. We seek to point the way to a new life in this land, established on principles of equality and love. We underline that any resolution must be based on the common good of all who live in this land without distinction.

We call on Christians in Palestine-Israel to join their voices with Jews, Muslims, Druze and all others, who share this vision of a society based on equality and the common good. We invite all to build bridges of mutual respect and love. The proposal for a two-state solution has gone nowhere and is repeated to no avail. In fact, all talk of political solutions seems empty rhetoric in the present situation.

Therefore, we promote a vision according to which everyone in this holy land has full equality – the equality befitting all men and women created equal in God's own image and likeness. We believe that equality is a fundamental condition for a just and lasting peace, whatever the political solutions that might be adopted.

We have lived together in this land in the past. Why should we not live together in the future, too?

150

This is our vision for Jerusalem and the whole land called Israel and Palestine located between the Jordan River and the Mediterranean Sea.

The Catholic Ordinaries of the Holy Land

This statement is included here, although it was signed by the members of the Assembly of Catholic Ordinaries of the Holy Land.

17. Restoring Property to Original Owners
(June 29, 2019)

At the end of March 2019, the Sabbagh family was issued with another eviction order from their home in the Sheikh Jarrah quarter in East Jerusalem. The Sabbaghs were refugees from Jaffa, losing their own home in the 1948 war. They moved into their present home in 1956 with the permission of the Jordanian authorities. This home had been abandoned by its Jewish residents in 1948 and the Sabbaghs took up residence as part of an agreement between the Jordanian authorities and the United Nations' agency for Palestinian refugees, UNWRA. The Jordanian authorities agreed to register the Sabbaghs as legal owners of their new residence in return for the Sabbaghs forfeiting their UNWRA recognition as refugees. The Sabbaghs forfeited their UNRWA recognition, but the registration was never completed.

The Sabbagh story is not uncommon. More stories like this one have come to light as Israelis lay claim to properties originally owned or once rented by Jews throughout the territories occupied by Israel after the 1967 war. This story has repeated itself, especially in East Jerusalem and Hebron, as Israeli settler associations, regularly supported by the State of Israel and backed up by Supreme Court rulings, seize those properties, many of which had become homes to Palestinian refugees after the 1948 war.

The restoration of properties to their original owners is a sound principle both in terms of international law, ethical principles and Church teaching. Those who were either evicted or because of circumstance were forced to flee, remain the legal owners of properties rightfully acquired. The return of their property conforms to the respect of the right to own property and furthers the common good. The Church teaches that "private property and other forms of private ownership of goods assure a person a highly necessary sphere for the exercise of his personal and family autonomy and ought to be considered as an extension of human freedom ... stimulating exercise of responsibility, it constitutes one of the conditions for civil liberty." (Compendium of the Social Doctrine of the Church, 176)

However, in the name of justice, if this principle is applied in some cases, it should be applied in other cases, too. If Jewish properties are restored to their rightful owners, who were divested of their rightful ownership in 1948, then Palestinian properties in West Jerusalem and elsewhere, lost by Palestinian owners in the course of the tragic events of 1948, must also be restituted to their rightful owners.

In the name of justice, we must condemn the evictions of families from homes they have lived in for decades when this is done not in order to restore justice, but rather to further a policy of facilitating the implantation of Israeli settlements in Palestinian neighborhoods and evicting Palestinians from their homeland. In fact, the disputed properties are most of the time not being returned to their original owners. Most of the time, they are being handed over to State-supported settler organizations that seek to transform the character of East Jerusalem and other Palestinian areas. The Church teaches that "the Church's social doctrine requires that ownership of goods be equally accessible to all, so that all may become, at least in some measure, owners, and it excludes recourse to forms of common and promiscuous dominion." (Compendium of the Social Doctrine of the Church, 176)

Therefore, the Justice and Peace Commission draws attention to the obligation of equally applying one law to Israelis and Palestinians alike. Equality and justice cannot be one-sided. Basic justice for all, without distinction, is an essential foundation for real and lasting peace.

Annex
Statutes of the Justice and Peace Commission
Assembly of Catholic Ordinaries of the Holy Land
(May 26, 2016)

Preamble

The Justice and Peace Commission (henceforth JPC) of the Assembly of Catholic Ordinaries of the Holy Land (henceforth ACOHL) was established by a letter from Cardinal Jean Villot, Secretary of State to Archbishop Pio Laghi, Apostolic Delegate in Jerusalem, on March 24, 1971, which authorized the establishment of this commission.

1. Nature of the Commission

The JPC is officially recognised by the ACOHL and functions under its auspices according to the mandate received and described hereafter. The inspiration for the JPC is to be found in the motuproprio *"Iustitiam et Pacem"* (10 December 1976): *"examining and studying (from the point of view of doctrine, pastoral practice and apostolate) problems connected with justice and peace, with the aim of awakening God's people to full understanding of these questions and awareness of the part they play and of the duties that fall on them in the fields of justice, the development of peoples, human advancement, peace, and human rights."* (§ I) Furthermore, the JPC is guided by the Pastoral Plan adopted by the Synod of the Catholic Churches in the Holy Land, with special reference to the 2000 document, *"The Presence of Christians in Public Life."*

2. Mandate and Mission

The JPC serves as a "think tank" to help the Ordinaries, the clergy, the religious and the laity to reflect on issues pertaining to justice and peace in the Catholic dioceses of the Holy Land. It also seeks to raise the consciousness of the Universal Church with regard to issues affecting the Church in the Holy Land. The mandate of the JPC covers two main areas.

a. Monitoring the political, social and economic situation in the Holy Land and the Middle East with special attention to human rights and a focus on issues connected to occupation, discrimination and inequality.

b. Monitoring the situation of Christians in the Holy Land with special attention to the social, political, economic and cultural challenges Christians face in the Holy Land and throughout the region. A special focus is the relations between Christians and Muslims, Christians and Jews and Christians and other religious minorities in the Holy Land and throughout the Middle East.

3. Work Method

The JPC holds regular meetings that focus on:

a. *Study*: The collection of information and the analysis of data that enables a coherent evaluation and understanding of policies and issues that are consistent with the teaching of the Church.

b. *Communication*: The transmission of information and analysis to the Ordinaries and other interested parties in the Local and Universal Church.

c. *Formation*: Assisting the Ordinaries in forming the people of God to meet the challenges faced in the field of justice and peace, where each one is called to respond according to the message of the Gospel and within the specific context of his/her life situation.

d. *Dialogue*: Working with individuals, institutions and political instances in order to establish channels of communication.

e. *Publication*: Composing brief statements that propose what the position of the Church is on issues related to justice and peace; statements that suggest analysis, discourse and action within the context of the present situation.

4. Structure

The JPC is composed of between five and 20 members and is under the jurisdiction of the ACOHL.

a. *President*: The AOCHL mandates the new President, one of the JPC members or someone who is not a member, after consulting the outgoing President and the members of the commission.

b. *Secretary*: The President appoints a secretary who convenes the meetings and records the proceedings that are circulated to the members of the JPC and to the members of the ACOHL.

c. *Members*: The members are nominated by the President to join the Commission. The members of ACOHL are encouraged to propose names as are other members of the JPC.

d. *Meetings*: The secretary convenes monthly meetings that are attended by all members. The agenda of the meeting is determined by the President and the members.

e. *Statements*: Statements released by the JPC must first be submitted to all members of the ACOHL. The members of the ACOHL have the responsibility to review these statements and can propose corrections, amendments or changes in the formulation within a period of three days.

f. *Report*: A yearly report should be drawn up by the Secretary and submitted to the members of the ACOHL at one of their bi-annual gatherings.

g. *Address*: The JPC has its seat in the office of the Secretariat of the ACOHL at Notre Dame de Jerusalem Centre.